LEAVING THE REST

GAY MEN ON ALCOHOLISM, ADDICTION, AND RECOVERY

EDITED BY LESLIE L. SMITH

Table of Contents

A.A. and Gay A.A.
An Introduction

Leslie L. Smith

Alcoholism is a major problem in the United States, according to the Centers for Disease Control. Some studies state that forty-five percent of all American families have at least one alcoholic family member. Estimates from Alcoholics Anonymous seem to support this. And its own popularity would underline that, too: There are 57,905 active A.A. groups in the U.S., which usually each have several meetings a week. Some of these groups offer as many as twenty meetings or more in a week. There are reportedly more than 1.2 million active members of A.A. in the U.S., and more than 2 million active members worldwide.

Alcoholism affects the LGBT community as well. Studies of the LGBT community since the early 1970s suggest that thirty percent of the U.S. gay population might have a problem with alcohol (though many of these studies have been criticized as being over-inflated). Researchers in some of these studies were accused of doing things such as drawing their subjects from within bars. An April 2010 report entitled "Healthy People 2010:

Companion Document for Lesbian, Gay, Bisexual, and Transgender Health," published with the cooperation of the Gay & Lesbian Medical Association, stated, "Early research on substance abuse among lesbians and gay men reported alarmingly high rates of drinking and other drug use." But the report also noted that these studies were misleading due to their reliance on extremely small, non-representative sample groups.

A.A. itself does not identify the problem within the gay community. It has no opinion on homosexuality—it is an "outside" issue. Therefore, A.A. does not publish statistics on the number of gay meetings, nor does it offer any reliable information on how often they are attended. This is true of all of A.A.'s "special-topic" or "special-interest" meetings. A.A. keeps its focus where it should, on its own message. It does not concentrate on the special needs of any one community. It instead allows communities to empower themselves in their own use of A.A. through these special-interest meetings.

As difficult as the extent of alcoholism in the gay community can be to quantify, it is much easier to qualify. We can gather a few facts that suggest A.A. and other such twelve-step meetings are common in gay communities. At the time of publication of this book, the Lesbian, Gay, Bisexual, and Transgender Center of New York City offers almost seventy twelve-step meetings each week, divided (almost equally) between either A.A. or Crystal Meth Anonymous. Thirty-some-odd city blocks away, a gay sober clubhouse in the theater district offers twelve meetings a day, seven days a week.

In Ft. Lauderdale, Fla., a similar sober clubhouse offers more than sixty gay-centric twelve-step recovery meetings each week. It is less than five miles away from the Pride Center, which also offers more than twenty-four such meetings each week. Only one of these weekly meetings is a women's group, and the majority of attendance at most meeting is generally known to be male. In spite of this, there is very little non-academic literature that speaks to being a gay man and being sober in or out of A.A.

But much is known about A.A. as a whole. It was founded in 1937, by Bill Wilson and Dr. Bob Smith. It was created with the intent of empowering alcoholics to "cure themselves." This radical and remarkable concept changed the lives of millions of those afflicted with what would later become known as the "disease" of alcoholism, as well as the friends, families, and co-workers of those individuals. According to A.A.'s official preamble, "Alcoholics Anonymous is a fellowship of men and women who share their experience, strength, and hope with each other so that they may solve their common problem." That common problem is, of course, an unhealthy relationship with alcohol and sometimes other substances.

The birth of A.A. is a milestone in the development of the fields of psychology and human behavior. But A.A.'s founders did not use the word *disease* to describe their condition at first. The first known use of the word disease as it relates to A.A. refers to the general "dis-ease" with life felt by many with alcohol issues. That concept, along with subsequent American Psychological Association and American Medical Association dual diagnoses of alcoholism, evolved into the commonly held idea that alcoholism is a disease.

The founders of A.A. first described alcoholism as an allergy, and said that like any allergy, those who suffered needed to avoid the substance to which they were allergic. Wilson and Smith also created social support networks to help break the habits associated with regular use of alcohol. In these support networks, the idea that the members had a disease was a popular one, and A.A. members lobbied the AMA for a diagnosis throughout the late 1940s and early '50s. It was finally given that status in 1956.

Today medical and psychological communities have two diagnoses for alcoholism: One is "dependence" and one is "abuse." The primary difference can be boiled down to this: Those who are dependent may require hospitalization to detox safely. But as a general rule, the treatment for each type is the same, abstinence. And for the majority of Americans, the best place to learn to abstain is through A.A. Alcoholism had a single diagnosis until 1991, when the two classifications were added under the definition. To this day no official diagnostic tool exists for either classification of alcoholism. The closest thing we have to such a tool is A.A.'s conventional wisdom, which says, "If you think you might be, you probably are."

As a guiding tool for those entering A.A., Dr. Bob and Bill Wilson wrote "The Twelve Steps of Alcoholics Anonymous." These became the foundation of what is known as the Program and provided the basis for a series concrete actions that empowered a chronic user to abstain from substance use. As part of keeping themselves sober, A.A.'s founders felt their personal success was only sustainable if they spent time helping others like themselves. In the process of curing themselves, "Bill W." and "Dr. Bob" would recruit a group of men and women, called "the first 100," who wanted to change their lives and to live sober. These 100 men and women would carry the message of A.A. throughout the country, and affect over the course of a single generation the way the entire world felt about people who have or had issues with alcohol.

The success of A.A. members who had managed to "heal themselves" would become a model for the treatment of other addictions and addictive behaviors, such as over-eating and gambling. The principles and practices of these programs have affected the development of therapy, mental-health diagnosis, and even medical treatment modalities. Quite simply, modern medicine would look quite different if not for A.A., Bill W., Dr. Bob, and the first 100.

The first 100 were nearly all upper-middle class American Christians, in a time before cultural sensitivity was widely practiced. They tried to design a program for everyone, but their work was clearly colored by their own beliefs, experiences, concerns and the time in which the program was created and the literature of A.A. written. They could only write what they knew firsthand, so the text of A.A., the Twelve Steps, and the Program are perhaps inadvertently filled with Judeo-Christian values and mores.

Although no two A.A. groups are alike, A.A. has an organizational structure that unites all of them (see Appendix A). The program of A.A. uses three principle tools to achieve this self-healing. They are:

1. **The Twelve Steps and the Twelve Traditions**: These provide the alcoholic with a spiritually based guide for living a sober life.
2. **The Fellowship**: This term refers principally to regular group meetings, but it also applies to social activities outside "the Program" with other recovering alcoholics. Fellowship is also often referred to as the program (with no capital). Meetings often feature a speaker who tells his or her own personal journey to and through A.A. Within a given group, a member is encouraged to choose a "sponsor," a personal guide through the rhetoric, the Fellowship, and the steps. The criterion for sponsorship is always a personal choice negotiated between the "sponsor" and "sponsee."

3. **The Literature**: The Program has two primary texts, *Alcoholics Anonymous* and *The Twelve Steps and the Twelve Traditions*.

Among the literature, the primary text is *Alcoholics Anonymous*, also known as the "Big Book." It is the official Program text of A.A. This 570-page book tells the story of A.A. and gives an overview of the steps. The first 164 pages outline the birth of A.A., it purpose, and the steps. It is commonly held among members that if it can't be found in the first 164 pages of the book, then it is not A.A. Everything not in print here is therefore someone's "opinion." The remainder of the book features "representative" personal stories of members, in which personal "experience, strength, and hope" are shared. Through four editions of *Alcoholics Anonymous*, however, these stories have not changed very much, and they do not include anything that speaks specifically to the gay experience of A.A. (even if one or two narrators in later editions mention being gay). These stories are much like the ones contained in this book.

The supplemental text, *The Twelve Steps and the Twelve Traditions*, is a twenty-four-chapter book, each dedicated to exploring one of the steps and traditions in more detail. It outlines the purpose and the context of each step and tradition for use in the process of getting sober and practicing the Program. The steps and traditions are found in Appendix B and Appendix C of this book, respectively.

Taken together, these tools make up what members call the "Program," and anyone seeking to stop drinking is encouraged to take the actions and suggestions contained within them. As one would imagine, members employ them with varying degrees of success.

There is a joke in A.A. about members who are doing what's called the "third-step waltz." This joke suggests that some members never achieve their full potential because they spend their sober experience only working steps one through three. This process counts off like a waltz, 1, 2, 3 … 1, 2, 3 … 1, 2, 3 …. This joke is born in a natural part of the Program's structure. The steps can be broken down into four sets of three as follows:

Steps 1 - 3: Admitting the need for help and choosing to believe help exists, usually in the form of God or a "Higher Power," and then, in turn asking for that help.

Steps 4 - 6: Chronicling, understanding, and accepting the "wreckage" of one's past, as it was created by drinking and/or using.

Steps 7 - 9: Cleaning up that "wreckage" in a direct and responsible way. This involves making direct amends to others for one's behavior while drinking or using.

Steps 10 - 12: Developing and maintaining a more responsible and reparative approach to daily life, including providing members with tools that help one to reflect and meditate on his or her own choices and behavior, as well as to address issues relating to all relationships in a proactive and healthy way.

As the aforementioned joke implies, it is true that many in the program can achieve some success by working just the first three steps. The power of "coming to believe" can carry many people a long way. But this, as the saying goes leads, to "sober horse thieves." For the Program to truly change one's life—and the way one relates to the world—the deeper, harder, scarier work of steps four through twelve is required. If one does the harder work, the Program promises results, which the Big Book says will begin to come true upon the completion of Step Nine:

7

If we are painstaking about this phase of our development we will be amazed before we are half way through. We are going to know a new freedom and a new happiness. We will not regret the past nor wish to shut the door on it. We will comprehend the word serenity and we will know peace. No matter how far down the scale we have gone, we will see our experience can benefit others. The feeling of uselessness and self-pity will disappear. We will lose interest in selfish things and gain interest in our fellows. Self-seeking will slip away. Our whole attitude and outlook on life will change. Fear of economic insecurity will leave us. We will intuitively know how to handle situations that used to baffle us. We will suddenly realize that God is doing for us what we could not do for ourselves. Are these extravagant promises? We think not. They are being fulfilled among us—sometimes quickly— sometimes slowly. They will always materialize if we work for them (83-84).

In spite of the suggested amount of step-work and the promises made, success in an A.A. fellowship is generally measured only by consecutive sober time. In most A.A. fellowships, this "sober" time is not only meant as a measurement of abstinence from alcohol, but also from any other mind- or mood-altering substance that might be taken without the express direction of a physician. In other words, painkillers prescribed after oral surgery would usually be considered acceptable, if used as directed (or even better, with less frequency and duration than prescribed). But if there are leftovers that are later used to treat a headache, then the member has "slipped." The principle of abstinence is generally applied to recreational drugs, but some members believe it should also be applied to anti-depressants, anti-psychotics, doctor-prescribed sleep aids, or other medically required substances, as these fall into a program defined class of "mind- or mood-altering substances." The culture of A.A. can sometimes be so rigorous that some members will often attempt minor surgeries without anesthetic for fear of triggering a "slip."

Officially, A.A. has "no opinion on outside issues" which, according to the text, includes the use of substances other than alcohol. But in this area, any new member of A.A., commonly called a "newcomer," would begin to notice discrepancies between the message of the "Fellowship" and the "text" of the program. Every meeting and fellowship activity is full of varied member opinions on the use of other chemicals, with most groups considering the use any substance not prescribed by a doctor as a "slip" or "relapse," even though the program's literature states "the only requirement for membership is a desire to stop drinking."

Most fellowships ask members to identify as a "newcomer" each time they slip. Any use of a mind- or mood-altering substance, at any time not subject to the direction and supervision of a doctor, restarts the clock on sober time. In many groups this "re-start" involves standing in the meetings and publicly counting these "sober" days until ninety days is achieved. In some places this "counting days" process is practiced up to the first year. This restart is generally expected by program members regardless of the amount of time achieved, or the substances used. For many, the process of "slipping" and starting over can become a debilitating and demoralizing cycle that goes on for years. But since all of A.A. is managed on the honor system, many members have altered these high standards to accommodate their own habits and stumbles from the ideal. These topics are often debated in the "rooms," i.e., any room where an A.A. meeting takes place, and this is often the subject of splintering within a particular group. Many groups, in meetings, have adopted a policy of discouraging "cross-talk," or responding to the content of another person's share, in order to prevent such heated debates.

Most fellowships have a night when they celebrate "birthdays" or "anniversaries" (depending on the regional name for the occasion). These celebrations mark the passage of a year of continuous sobriety. The group usually sets these nights aside as special occasions. People with a decade or more of continuous sobriety are lauded for their achievement, and often considered sages, in spite of whatever difficult realities lay behind their success in working the steps.

The Program's messages and applications vary from region to region and even group to group. This malleability makes it difficult to say what A.A. "is." In spite of being well organized internationally, the local nature of governance means that even the most basic of expected structures, such as rules for punctuation and the correct grammatical use of terms, can vary from group to group.

An example of this is the actual timeline of step work. In their original application, the steps were worked successively, in a 24- to 48-hour period, in a hotel room, while detoxing. Today, some groups still argue that success in A.A. depends on a swift and thorough execution of the steps. Other groups may say that working one step a year makes for a slow and steady recovery. Many times these varied philosophies will be found within the context of a single group, and differing opinions lead to divisions into clique-like circles that make for heated group politics. Much of this political heat centers around discussions of what A.A. "is" and what it "is not." And just as Protestant factions splintered over time after the initial departure from Catholicism, various forms and versions of twelve-step programs have adapted for treating other addictions the literature that A.A. developed, in large part because A.A. would label such discussion as an "outside issue." Among these groups are Narcotics Anonymous and Crystal Meth Anonymous, two group meetings that are also widely known in gay sober circles. Each of these various "splinter" groups is a twelve-step program, which its members refer to as "the Program."

This variance is perhaps best regarded in what may be the most universally applied A.A. slogan. It tells members to "Take what you need—and leave the rest." Twelve-steppers, perhaps more than anyone, know that not all they prescribe will work for all people. This is why a "group consciousness" drives the governance of each individual meeting.

In spite of its tremendous malleability, there are a few common ideas that will be found in almost every A.A. meeting:

1. Sobriety requires total abstinence from alcohol and recreational drugs.
2. Sobriety is best achieved on a spiritual (God-centric) path, though it is possible to be agnostic and achieve sobriety.
3. Alcoholism is an addiction, and addiction is a life-threatening disease, one that ultimately claims the lives of many users and many in the fellowship.

In spite of the program's success, for many in this world it may also be true that sobriety—defined as total abstinence from mood-altering substances—is not really the best answer. Some "sober" people rely on doctor-prescribed mood stabilizers, some have issues with one substance but not another, some gay men use amyl nitrate or ethyl chloride during sex but don't drink or use drugs, and some sober gay men have secret "slip weekends" on the gay party circuit. Others, after an extended period of sobriety, find they can leave the program and use with some normalcy. Still others leave the twelve-step room but use what they learned to stay sober.

Many people committed to the program shun these alternative life choices, sure that any use of mind and mood-altering substances is a developmental step backward—and any step away from the program is a step toward using. If you choose to step outside A.A's model and define sobriety differently than complete abstinence, there are not many places to seek help. Such choices are often looked on with distain or negative peer pressure from the true twelve-step devotees.

Beyond offering members the option to "leave the rest," the program has not evolved much since it was first conceived. Even the seemingly inclusive "We Agnostics" chapter of the Big Book states that while people can stay sober without finding God, it also suggests that such people will not find all the benefits offered by the Program and its promises. In this chapter's last few sentences, it is suggested that eventually, the practice of the steps will give every person who wants sobriety a God: "Some of us grow into it more slowly" (57).

The issue of anonymity, and what it means, has been another commonly debated topic in A.A since the beginning. Anonymity is not one of the steps. The Program's most basic statements regarding anonymity are contained in *The Twelve Traditions*. The Eleventh Tradition reads, "Our public relations policy is based on attraction rather than promotion; we need always maintain personal anonymity at the level of press, radio, and films." And the Twelfth Tradition states, "Anonymity is the spiritual foundation of all our traditions, ever reminding us to place principles before personalities."

Most of A.A.'s literature about anonymity is focused on the public image of the group. A.A. hopes that the success of the many will never be tied to the public image of a few individuals, especially those who might fail at the journey of life-long sobriety, which A.A. admittedly knows to be a tall order. The prefaces to the first two editions of *Alcoholics Anonymous* each speak to the role of anonymity in managing the group's response to an overwhelming amount of publicity and an unmanageable growth, and the need to place the group's message ahead of any individual in the spotlight.

A.A.'s official chapter on the Twelfth Tradition is found in *The Twelve Steps and the Twelve Traditions*. It speaks about protecting A.A. from questionable publicity generated by individuals who may undercut its values. It clearly asks, "How anonymous should an A.A. member be?" The book discusses the organization's long debate on the topic. In the end, in spite of its own writings on the topic, most A.A. members hold anonymity to be a "spiritual tenet" of the Program, one that many still deem vital to any individual's success in the program. A.A.'s official statement on a member's choice to be public can be found in the pamphlet "A.A. Facts":

An A.A. member may, for various reasons, "break anonymity" deliberately at the public level. Since this is a matter of individual choice and conscience, the Fellowship as a whole obviously has no control over such deviations from tradition. It is clear, however, that such individuals do not have the approval of the overwhelming majority of members.

When it comes to gay men, there might be a need for re-thinking the Program as it presents itself, including the use of anonymity. Gay men are commonly more mobile than heterosexuals, better educated, and more likely to rebel against social norms than the average non-gay member of A.A. Gay men also have their own sub-cultures. Each is a more complex and modern culture than that of A.A.'s at its founding. Rightly or wrongly, substance use in gay culture can be our rite of passage, socially bonding us as men in our tribe. It is, sometimes *our thing*. It can be easy for anyone to get lost in that part of gay culture and to lose sight of the negative impact using these substances can have, especially when they are associated with such emotionally charged experiences as coming out and discovering sexuality. I think that this experience is why much of gay culture still centers on bars and circuit parties, in spite of all the political and social advances we have made.

While many of us may associate our sexual freedoms with our parties, others associate drinking and drug use with the shame of the closet, stuffing unwanted desires into a bottle. For these men, using can empower them through internalized homophobia and self-hate, a cycle few manage to overcome once it starts. Whatever the case, there is no doubt many gay men often approach substance use differently than straight men. As such, they might need to approach sobriety differently as well. A few out, sober role models might be a good thing for our community.

I can't speak to why some contributors to this book have chosen to reveal their identities, while others chose not to. I can only speak to why I gave them the opportunity to do so. A.A.'s Twelfth Tradition was the only place that A.A. told me what I was to believe. The rest of the program said my spiritual life was my own, and that I was free to explore, express, and examine it without influence from the program. A.A. has always said I could believe in anything, as long as I believed in something that empowered me. But in the Twelfth Tradition it also said that I must believe anonymity was a spiritual foundation of my program's success.

My sexuality and my use of substances were linked from the time I accepted my first beer at my first gay party. After hearing countless gay members of A.A. share their story over more than twenty years, I can say that many gay men experience a developmental link between coming out and discovering their sexuality and the use of alcohol or other chemical substances. In turn, so was my sobriety linked to my sexuality, in complex ways it would take me decades to fully grasp. But my sexuality is also linked to an "Out Loud and Proud" ideal, one that I could never manage to reconcile with the anonymous nature of twelve-step programs.

Leaving the Rest is about that complex gay sober experience. It is not a book about getting sober, though those stories are to be found here. This book is meant to explore the bell-curve of recovery, the range of stories that includes the many successful twelve-step versions, and some variations on that traditional view. But like all samples, the bell curve is not fully comprehensive or fully representative of what it means to be a gay man in recovery.

The book is not only meant for those who are embarking on the twelve-step journey for the first time; it is also for those who are or have been in the program. It is also for those people who care for gay alcoholics, as family members or as health care providers. This is a book about understanding what it is to live sober as gay men over time, or, in some cases, as sober as possible. It is meant to help us rediscover and celebrate our differences, both as people who suffer from "addictive" behaviors and as gay individuals. *Leaving the Rest* is meant to help gay men wrestling with questions of addiction to think about how they might best approach their own lives and their own recovery path. It is meant to inspire gay men to follow that most inner voice, the one that tells us all what we must do to be happy. Finally, it is meant to empower any gay man, anywhere, who is struggling with these questions, at any point in his life.

Dolly Would
Jim B.

I took my first drink my first weekend at college. It was a pink wine cooler. My future was written in that drink: I would be a gay alcoholic. Until that first taste, though, I was still a virgin, to both men and liquor. The drink won me first, the men would come later, and in the middle would come Dolly Parton.

I was the Most Innocent of my high school class. I was the obedient child. I never made waves or looked for trouble. I earned good grades and played the violin. What I didn't understand then was that I wasn't a golden boy; I was merely paralyzed by fear, afraid of just about everything. People, places, and things? Pshaw! That was just the beginning; I mostly feared myself. What fear did not conquer, the relentless command "No, you can't" finished off the rest. Squished between Fear and Can't, I didn't stand a chance.

It was the early eighties. The eve of my adolescence coincided with the eve of AIDS. I feared my body and I feared sex. Picked on for being skinny and beaten up for being a homo, I hated my body and I misunderstood my sexuality long before I even knew what it was. I thought that sex would bring AIDS, and AIDS would bring shame, and AIDS would bring death.

So I hid. I hid from my body and I hid from being

gay. I evacuated my body and escaped into my mind, oblivious to anything and everything from the neck down. Back then, before King Alcohol, Fear, and Can't gave me refuge, they kept me away from men and sex. They wrapped me up tightly and hid me behind thick walls. Safe and sound. They protected me. I could not see, let alone imagine, a way out, and that suited me just fine. I wanted no part in letting the genie out of the bottle. That is, until I found alcohol.

Alcohol freed the genie. Or perhaps it would be better to say that alcohol began to let me out, a little bit at a time, and it kept me on a very short leash. I would let some alcohol in and alcohol would let some of me out; that was our deal. Alcohol was the magic potion that fixed me in ways I did not know I was broken.

The drink loosened up this skinny boy from the cornfields. Alcohol let me joke for the first time, alcohol let me write for the first time. Alcohol helped me see who I could be, and it was such a surprise to discover who had been hiding inside. This wallflower began to blossom and step out from the wallpaper. As I stepped into life, people began to notice me for the first time. I began to make friends; professors told me that I had ideas, that I had promise. Alcohol opened a door; it gave me a taste of my personality. But back then, life was easy and drinks were fun. White Russian, Black Russian, Bloody Mary, Burgundy, Blue Kamikaze, and white Zinfandel, I wanted to try all the colors. During those college years, alcohol was working; it was part of the solution. Alcohol opened me up and made me bigger in many ways. It showed me I could be strong and vibrant, it took away so many fears, but not all of them, just some. I loved alcohol, it was my friend, even better than a friend because alcohol never let me down, or so I thought. I had no idea then that it was already in the process of betraying me.

What I could not admit in those early days was that I was gay. Alcohol helped me find my beginnings with that one, too. Drunk one lonely Friday night my freshman year, I came out to myself. Maudlin as it was, it was a start. At seventeen, pain pushed me out of the closet, but not into bed or the arms of a man. I realize now that this was the first time I got drunk alone. It is no surprise that the lines of emergent sexuality and alcohol met that night; the sad truth is they met that night and remained hopelessly intertwined for another twenty years.

I began a two year Master's program that took me over six years to complete (I can be tenacious, if anything). During those years, life got harder, and King Alcohol's potion turned subtly sour. Those were desperate days. I so wanted to finish that degree, to write that thesis, but I could not figure out what to do or where to start. Just as much, I desperately wanted to have sex and love a man and be loved, but like that thesis, I could not figure out how to do any of it. Life was such a mystery in those dark days of my twenties. My psyche had become some kind of complicated playing field. The ball was always in the air, but it never really went anywhere, or at least I certainly did not. I just spun in circles. Those were the days of *some* alcohol and *much* "-ism." In a nutshell, I was officially a mess.

At the end of my twenties, I went back to school and landed in Paris. There, I mark the beginning of my proverbial bottom. In France, without friends, family, and cultural expectations (read, limitations and boundaries), I was free and had a paycheck, so I drank and drank and drank. I could drink because I had no witnesses and yet I drank because I was so terribly lonely. I was desperate for an intimacy that I did not know and a human touch that I would not allow myself to have. That was my bottom, and I dragged and bumped along that bottom until I finally quit drinking seven years later.

In the gray wet winter of Paris 2007, I realized I was done. I got sober. It was the first day of spring.

Flash forward almost six years and my life has changed little on the outside. Same address, same job, just less hair. On the inside, much has changed. My fears are slipping away and so, too, are the resentments. Fear and Can't are losing power, although they do like to pop in now and then to ruin my day. In sobriety, I have accepted my body, and I have come to love its flaws. I have embraced my sexuality and Fear and Can't no longer hold me paralyzed; I now enjoy a healthy sex life (and wink, wink, so do the men who love me). Once dark and grumpy, I now smile and make people laugh. I used to hide my eyes, now I look up with them and smile with a sparkle; I can smile at myself. When I drank, I wore only black, now I only wear colors. I used to wear baggy clothes to hide my skinny body, now I wear tight jeans because quite frankly, they make me look good. I know freedom now; I am no longer dependent on alcohol. I no longer run in fear, now I walk in ease, I walk in joy. I have made peace with my past and I no longer fear the future. I remember insanity and I remember anger, but now I know serenity and now I know peace. I am no longer hopeless, now I help others and have hope for them and hope for myself. It is no longer a question of half full or half empty, nowadays, the glass is full, period. The unknown future no longer troubles me like it used to, everything will unfold following divine order, and I will receive my divine orders; I always do.

I have all this now. How did I do it? How did I get it? What's my secret? In a word: Dolly. In two words: Dolly Parton.

But I'm getting ahead of myself. That first year, I worked exclusively with a therapist. A year later I knew I needed something more, a new plan. I decided I would *try* Alcoholics Anonymous. I figured that with almost a year of sobriety under my belt, I was already sober, fixed and cured, so in order to keep me interested it would have to be really good, it would have to knock my socks off. So I went, but with the stipulation that I would *test* it, for the summer. I was not signing up for the lifetime plan; I wanted to take it for a test drive, let's call it "summer school." More importantly if I had to go, it would have to be *gay A.A.* The least I could do for myself was to find my gay tribe.

At that first meeting, two critical things happened. A guy said, "When I drank, my life was about alcohol. Now that I'm sober, my life is about what I want it to be." I knew he was on to something, but I wanted to know exactly what he was on *to.* After the meeting when the guy next to me realized that it was my first meeting, he advised me, *Take from it what you want.* He gave me permission to question; I needed that. Those two men baited and hooked me; they had me at hello—hook, line, and sinker—and I didn't even see it coming.

So it began. I went in seeking protection from alcohol, and I found it in bits and pieces, in unexpected shapes and forms. Those bits and pieces became the paving stones of and toward my spiritual path.

Fortunately, though, I did not realize any of this at the beginning. I did not want God, I did not want some "higher power," I did not want half of the stuff written on those walls; I came because I wanted peace, I came because I wanted to stay sober.

The first piece I picked up was the Serenity Prayer. For me, the Serenity Prayer wasn't a prayer, it was a tool. The logic and axiomatic simplicity of those words appealed to my strong sense of reason straightaway (how could anything logical like that be a prayer, anyway?).

There are things that I can change, and there are things I cannot change. If I cannot change them, I have to accept them. If I can change them, then I must change them. To this beginner, that wasn't a prayer, that was *a flow chart*; I loved it and I used it all the time.

Even though I scooped up the Serenity Prayer early on, I resisted practically every other aspect of the program those first months. That said, I still went, every Tuesday night. Alcoholics Anonymous is undeniably the greatest show in town, and I went for the show, for the stories, for the people. I went back because I wanted to find out how the stories would turn out.

During that A.A. summer school, I met a woman named Georgia; she became my first friend in A.A., and she changed my life. Old enough to be my mother, and with over twenty years of sobriety, Georgia understood exactly how to handle this porcupine of a newcomer; she took me to dinner. With her partner, Catherine, we would have carry-out rotisserie chicken at their dining room table and talk gossip and program. Georgia told me one of those first nights, "Jimbo, you're in the right place."

What could be more ridiculous?! Never in my life had I been in the right place, and yet, wise Georgia knew and understood things far above my head. For as much as I wanted to resist and critique and disbelieve and deny, I knew I needed to shut up and to try to understand. Those words made me uncomfortable because they made me realize very deeply that not only had I never felt in the right place before, but I was not feeling so sure about where I was at that very moment. Even deeper, more pointedly, Georgia's declaration made me recognize that I had never felt as if I had ever *belonged* anywhere before.

For me, the thought of being in the right place constituted a radical shift in perspective. The lesson assured me that I was perfectly fine just the way I was, where I was. It took me a while to absorb this one (honestly, it took years). At first, all I could do was look at my feet and see where they were. All I could do was feel it in my feet. Neither my heart nor my mind could feel that rightness, so my legs and feet began the process. My heart and my mind eventually absorbed and accepted the validity of the message, and it slowly brought me confidence, which in turn slowed down my racing mind and slowed down my racing feet. This first lesson became the most powerful, and the most beautiful, spiritual lesson I have ever learned this far.

It first meant simply that I was physically in the right place, as in, not in front of a bottle of red wine. It did not take me long to understand that being in the right place was much deeper than my feet standing in the right place, that it was about divine order, and that there are no mistakes, there are no wrong answers, that there is no waste. This understanding brought me peace and helped me see the right where I had previously only seen the wrong. The idea helped me discover that there exists a natural order to the world and that I had a place in it. Being in the right place was just Georgia's spin on a spiritual law, she just used the vernacular.

As suggested in the program, I began writing gratitude lists. At first I balked, I scoffed, and served as a perfect example of contempt prior to investigation. *Gratitude List? What a ridiculous idea.* And then I wrote one. The practical beauty of gratitude hit me before I could write down the third item on my list. *Oh! I get it.* Discovering gratitude, I inched up five points on the humility scale and slid five spaces closer to God. Fortunately, again, still, I did not realize where I was heading.

Although it hurt my ego, in August of that year, I surrendered to the fact that I was not going to A.A. for "summer school" or even part-time, that I was in it for the long haul. Later, probably a year later, I finally admitted that I was an alcoholic (I was in no rush to come to any conclusions on the matter). I surrendered again and asked a man to sponsor me. I began working the steps. When I got to step three, I did not quite know what to do about the God issue (which makes me wonder how I got through step two).

As a young boy, I questioned Sister Rita Joan about Jesus being Jewish, and about the seat of Christianity being located in Rome and not Jerusalem. I was already on to The Church. Not much later, I figured out that men were fallible and that there was a difference between man-made laws and God-given laws. From there, it was just a short step to understand the clear and simple difference between religion and spirituality. At that young age, I did not yet have the word *spirituality*, but I knew there was something even bigger and better than religion. My precociousness spared God, but eliminated that Catholic Christian God; I had pretty much given him the boot.

Hence, I came into the rooms of A.A. as a lucky agnostic. I say lucky because I had no bone to pick with God, I did not hold him in contempt. God might make cancer or typhoons, but man has will, free will. Given his free will, man can take care of the ill and clean up after the typhoon *if he so chooses*. To me, in my tough love childhood home, it seemed abundantly clear that if we lived in a world with evil and sadness, it was most likely because man chose to make it so. He was neither friend nor foe nor ally, he was just God, a character in church and epic poetry.

At step three, I had no desire to change my thinking on the God question. But then again, I just didn't care. The God question was moot. Besides, I figured I'd do it all without God either way. But my sponsor insisted. I needed to have a God of my own understanding. I figured this God character of my youth would do until I found better, so I used him to mark the spot, to get me through until a new and improved version of God (or something, or whatever) came along. This became another powerful spiritual lesson, "Good Enough."

"Good Enough" would become my equivalent of "suit up and show up." Although I enjoyed the certitude of the announcement "half measures availed us nothing," I still contend that half measures certainly do avail us something. The trick with me was that as a perfectionist (which is just a kinder way of calling myself a control freak) I needed everything to be just so. Driven by Fear and Can't, I never managed to do anything, because I thought it had to be done perfectly. Step three caught me up. I knew that this God of my youth was imperfect, but for want of something better, I cut my losses, called that God "good enough" and moved on; I was in a beginner's rush to get through all the steps and win the prize at the end.

I did my first fourth step with that faux-God in the background and enjoyed wildly amazing liberating results. I'd like to say that this cardboard cut-out God was good enough to get me through the fifth step, and the sixth and the seventh, too. I'd like to say that this Faux-God carried me through the trials and tribulations of the early days, but that would not be true. Truth be told, that God of my youth sat in his heaven and played no real role in any of my steps, nor for that matter, did that God play any role in my life at all.

One evening, that all changed. I was walking home listening to Dolly Parton. I have always loved Dolly. She has always inspired me. Her laughter has always made me laugh. I always admired her deep faith and her sincere humility. Her generosity of spirit has always impressed me, her sense of humor has always made light of every situation (so much light!). Who could be more loving? More generous? More accepting? More creative? More spiritual? *She should be somebody's Higher Power,* I thought.

She's yours, announced a voice in my head. I balked and relented in the same motion. I knew that voice was right. It had already been decided; Dolly Parton was my Higher Power.

It was true. There was no retracting, no denying, no ifs, ands, butts, or boobs. Dolly. Parton. My. HP. Dolly.

And yet, as crazy as it all sounded, it made sense, and suddenly, all of it, it all began to make sense and align. A God of our own. A God of our understanding. A God of *our own understanding.* That is what it says in the Big Book, right? My sponsor's HP was a tree, why couldn't I have Dolly? I understand Dolly Parton. She is a bighearted, carefree, wonderful woman. I could talk to Dolly. I could tell her anything. Couldn't you? Moreover, what couldn't you tell Dolly Parton? She will listen and she will not judge, she will accept and she will understand, she will love, and she will love freely and she will love generously. She won't shake a finger, she'll listen, she'll hear your every word. I wanted a God I could sit and have a cup of coffee with. That's what I found, that's what I received. I said thank you.

I suddenly had that higher power people were talking about in meetings. I had that God that I read about in the literature. In the Big Book, Bill gives us permission to find a God that makes sense to us. To show us, he uses a number of words to describe that God: Father of light, spirit of the universe, creative intelligence, a God of our own understanding, and my favorite, a newfound friend.

That's what I found in Dolly. I could be completely honest with her. She was that newfound friend that I desperately needed. In the program, they tell us we don't have to do anything alone. I always had a hard time with that lesson; I always did everything alone. Who would want to help me? And why? Besides, they probably wouldn't help me anyway, right? Although I had begun to talk to people and I had begun to ask for help, I was doing it on my own, by myself. With Dolly in my life, I don't have to do anything alone anymore. I embraced the Buddy System (who knew it was a spiritual concept?), and took my God with me everywhere I went and I finally began to accept that I really was in the right place.

Mind you, for the record, I understand that Dolly Parton is not God. For me, I suppose, she is a kind of prophet. What I tell Dolly, she shares it with God, or something, I really don't know. I haven't spent too much time worrying about how the system works. I'm just an alcoholic; I'm not a theologian.

That evening walking home, I made an initial *conscious contact* with my Higher Power. That phrase from Step Eleven, *conscious contact*, had been floating around my imagination since my early days. But until that moment, that night, I had never quite grasped what *conscious contact* really meant. And then, suddenly, click, it came to me.

Conscious. Contact. Conscious, as in being aware, awake, or mindful. Or conscious, as in being deliberate, or intentional, or purposeful. Contact, as in touch, communication, or connection. I can play a game of Mix-n-Match with these words and create dozens of similar phrases to define conscious contact. Conscious is about waking up from our stupor and being aware, being mindful; it is about *feeling*, it is about *knowing*. Conscious also describes just quite *how* we make that contact. It does not happen by mistake, we make it *willfully*, we make it *deliberately*. Contact, finally, describes a state of touching, which implies that there is some *thing* or some *one* to touch; that one is God. (And mind you, one last twist, a contact can also be an acquaintance, an associate, or even a friend.) No matter how you slice it, contact always implies a relationship between two entities, and I had just been contacted by my newfound friend, and our new relationship was just beginning.

Suddenly, with my newfound friend, I had a far better understanding of God and what God was, because now I had one *of my own understanding.* With it, I realized what conscious contact was and how to do it; I just *talked* to her. That talk, quite simply, is prayer, or, the other way around, prayer is just talking to your God.

The next morning, I addressed my eleventh step to Dolly. So began our rich relationship. My higher power became my partner, my buddy. Finding my higher power, I expanded the Buddy System exponentially; I multiplied the Buddy System by the power of God. With my newfound friend, the quality of my life, and my sobriety, proceeded to improve considerably. (I use the word *considerably* here with great purpose. The word comes from the Latin meaning "examine" and comes from the words "con" meaning "with" and "sider" meaning "stars." With the arrival of my HP, I began to examine matters (like myself) earnestly, and found myself *among the stars*, or with that cosmic power, or, as they say, in the fourth dimension.)

So what happened? What changed?

If you know Dolly Parton, you know that she is incredibly loving and has a down home wisdom that cuts through the bullshit and the tears. I needed that love and I needed that wisdom, but mostly, I needed that psychic, cosmic, down home company.

As an alcoholic (and an introvert, to boot), I am happy to spend exorbitant amounts of time in my head.

Nothing happily numbs me more than watching an idea spin around and around my head. Dolly became my interlocutor and got me out of my head. She gave me someone to listen to besides myself. In the old days, I spoke to myself, I thought to myself, and my thoughts could only extend as far as I could take them (around and around the racetrack of my brain). With Dolly, I could talk to her, explain the situation to her, and inevitably, a bumper sticker Dolly truism would pop up and set me on the right track, which was good, because most of the time I was on the wrong track. She's a tough love woman, Dolly. She shaped up my ship.

Tough love, yes, but first, love. Dolly gave me the love that I desperately needed to find in myself. She offered me a gentleness that I could not offer myself. I have wrestled with how to describe this gift of love. Did Dolly show it to me? Did she give it to me? I'm not sure it was either. Perhaps her loving presence radiated love onto me the way the sun shines on plants? Perhaps it happened that way. I know that it was not an On/Off process, it was a gradual process. Perhaps I merely learned from Dolly's love and emulated it. Sometimes I wonder if it was even love she shone onto me. Maybe she imparted confidence or self-esteem? Whatever it was, I desperately needed it, because whatever it was, I certainly did not have much of it.

We all know that the elixir to hate is love, and Dolly offered me copious amounts of love. I needed it. Love brings peace, love brings security, love brings belonging. I needed that love and I needed those consequences of love. The funny thing is, I didn't even see the cure coming because in many ways I hadn't even seen the ailment. When I came into A.A., like everyone, I suppose, I suffered from the wounds of the past and the hurts of the present. I so needed to heal. Only much later did I learn that the hurtful events and painful moments of the past created the grammar to a language that I spoke in the present. They had so integrated into who I was that I no longer saw their structure, and yet, ignorant of their existence, they continued to grow into me, ever and ever thicker and stronger with the years.

Had you pointed out that self-loathing and asked me to heal it, I would have given it my all. I would have pulled out the hammers and the axes and chainsaws and set to work dismantling it. But it didn't happen that way. Instead, Dolly gave me softness and gentleness and like water to loose dirt, it washed away so much of that self hate. The process happened ever so gradually that I did not even know what was happening, or that anything was happening at all. It only became clear to me later in sobriety. In A.A., we would call this an example of *God doing for us what we could not do for ourselves.*

And therein lies yet another important lesson. I used to believe, heart and soul, that God only gave us what we could handle. Then one morning as I stumbled to the kitchen to pour myself a cup of ambition, I groaned aloud, "It takes an act of God to get me out of bed." The recognition of what I had said woke me up straightaway. With that admission, I realized that my thinking had been wrong; God gave me more than I could handle *all the time*. And so, yet again, I learned a new lesson and began turning toward the divine in my daily life, not just for the problems, but for the little stuff, like getting out of bed.

Not so very long ago I discovered another facet of the idea that "God is doing for us what we could not do for ourselves." We hear this phrase all the time in the rooms of A.A., but it had never occurred to me that this could be a quality that *my God* could possess. And so, suddenly, I wanted a God who would do for me what I could not do for myself. Before, HP was a friend, a *confidante.* With this new aspect, I endowed my God with superpowers. I have eyes on the front of my head; I want a God who has my back. I want a God who can see on the other side of the door, who can see what's going on behind me, I want a God who's going to cover me when I walk into the job interview, or the date, or Christmas dinner. I need a God like that, I *want* a God like that, because life is big and full of challenges.

The flip side to this lesson is, if God is going to do for me what I cannot do for myself, then I am obliged to do my part. God will do his/her/its part, and I have to do mine. God can make me a baseball superstar, but I have to pick up the bat and swing at the ball. I have to try. God will not hit the ball for me, that's my responsibility. This is that free will stuff I talked about earlier. And when I'm afraid (and we will get to fear), I have to walk through the fear and do it anyway. I have to swing at the ball, because God is only going to do his/her/its part. I gotta pick up that bat and swing. My God and I work together, as a team. I have to cooperate. For me, this is the essence of step three.

What I have learned is that the more I co-operate with God, the easier it all gets. I have learned to share my fears with God (that's what most people call a fourth step). The more I give away my fears, the more confident I become. In time, I have come to understand that many of my fears only existed in my imagination. Some of my fears disappeared quickly but others have been more persistent. As they have disappeared and diminished, I have come to appreciate that the opposite of fear is faith. As I eliminate fear, I make more room for faith, and the more I have faith means I have less room for fear. The effects are cumulative. It's that simple.

The more I cooperate with God, the better I understand what is happening around me. Why? Because I'm seeing more clearly. In the old days, I looked at life through fear colored glasses. Fear sat between me and life; fear sat between me and God. The less fear I have, the better I perceive what's happening in my life. The less fear I have the more life makes sense. As I began telling Dolly the stories of my day and those of the past and even those of the future, I began to see the connections and the patterns. I began to see where I was wrong and where I had done right. She helped me see the big picture.

I do none of this perfectly. But I have learned to do my part, I have learned "Good Enough." Just show up. Suit up, shut up, say your prayers, and show up. Most of the time, that qualifies for successful results. Happily, this lesson works at the gym, too.

What this all boils down to is faith. When I came into the rooms of Alcoholics Anonymous I did not believe in God and I had no faith. In time, as I watched the people around me getting better, living better, I began to trust that I could, too. The better ones worked the steps, the best ones practiced the steps and cultivated an intimate relationship with their higher power, and do so, everyday; they are the winners. I watched those people, I emulated them; I became their friend, and like them, I found a friend in my higher power, who helped me become a winner, too.

Faith does not come easily, though. The old adage is true: faith without works is dead. To me, that means that faith is not free, it does not fall out of the sky. We have to work at it, and it will come to us. Although the expression is *to have faith*, we never own faith or truly possess it (that said, nobody can take it away from us, either, now can they?). The best we can do is to hold faith—and hold it carefully.

I have learned that Faith is action, it is something we *do*. Faith is really a verb; we trust, we hope, we believe. Faith results from action; faith is a consequence. Faith works similarly to a bicycle. A bicycle moves forward when I peddle; when I stop peddling, I stop moving and tip over. Hence, faith is something I practice and I have to practice it every day in order to stay upright and to keep moving forward.

Of course, having faith is not always as easy as riding a bike. It can be difficult having faith sometimes. Some days, I feel sad and lonely, I feel blue, some days I just don't want to turn it over, and some days I don't want to let it go, either. Some days, I want to manage my own finances, or I want to run my sex life my way. Mind you, by now I know that this is never a good idea and that I'm in the process of cutting off my own nose, but usually it's just that I *forget* to turn it over and to let it all go. Old habits die hard. Faith is a process, not a perfection, but a progression.

In time, I have come to understand that everything, all of it, is working. In sobriety, I have found that those "Ninth Step Promises" do come true. I have become a truly happy person. I enjoy living; I enjoy my life. More to the point, I *have* a life, a good life, a full life, an inner life, an outer life, filled with friends and family and fun, honest, real activities that count, that matter. I have learned to talk to people and I have learned to talk to myself. I have learned who I am, and I continue to discover what I can do. Now I can imagine what I can do next. In sobriety, those childhood walls around me have lowered, thinned. I have begun to deconstruct many of those rules that I had made up that hemmed me in and kept me safe. I have begun to realize that those rules came from me, not society or culture or my family. I no longer fear myself, I have come to see who I am, and realize that in fact I am not, I repeat, I am not an ugly kid or a boney kid or a fucking homo. Only lately have I begun to realize that the skinny dork in my mind currently resides in a solid, attractive, wide-shouldered body. I have confidence now, real confidence, based in self-knowledge and humility. In sobriety, I have accepted my body and my sexuality and now I celebrate them both, alone, and with others; I have become an excellent, warm, generous, passionate lover, a mere shadow of that cold board I used to be. I know now what I have, and what I have not, and I have accepted both; I have begun to accept myself, as I am, for what I am.

Quite simply, I have become a happy man and the Promises are coming true. They are coming true because Dolly could and would, if she were sought. And me, I seek. I can't afford not to, because I'm an alcoholic, my name is Jim.

Spoiled Little Boy Grows Up
N.H.W.

Growing up I saw repeatedly that drugs and alcohol could wreak havoc on people and their families, including my own. I was mostly raised by my grandparents, in large part because of my birth parents were unfit to raise me. I was warned by my grandparents that I should not drink and certainly not do drugs. Yet in spite of the problems I saw, all I focused on were the fun and glamour of being an adult who drank. I saw most of my relatives and their friends drinking, and they appeared cool. I equated drinking with being an adult and being cool. I wanted that because I was so uncool as a kid.

When I was fourteen, I decided I wanted to get away from home and my neighborhood. We had heard about a boarding school that had recently been given a large donation that provided scholarships. I asked my grandmother if I could go. It was one of the best things that happened in my life. Yet, there was a lot of freedom, and I grew up fast being away from home. I discovered pot; of course the cool kids introduced me to it. I desperately needed to feel better, and pot made me feel like I was a part of something exciting. But pot was not a big issue for me in high school. I didn't do it often enough, and I didn't even know how to inhale properly.

Alcohol, however, was different. I drank alcoholically

from the beginning, starting at fifteen. Even then, I did not have an off switch with alcohol. I drank until I fell down, passed out, or vomited. And it continued that way, off and on, until I got sober.

Fortunately, alcohol was hard to come by during my high school years. I only encountered it a handful of times. On one of those occasions, I was almost expelled from school, four days before graduation. One of my drinking companions urinated in the room of another student during a blackout. He thought he was in the bathroom. My drinking companion ended up getting expelled, and the school administration caught wind that we had been together. My dorm master came to my room while I was passed out and started a conversation. I sobered myself up immediately and pretended to be fine. I am sure I smelled like a distillery and my eyes were probably red as cherries, but he bought my story. Looking back, I think he probably gave me a pass because I was able to play along and it was so close to graduation.

The next day, I was summoned to the Dean's office for questioning along with another drinking companion. My enrollment at school was on the line, and I was not willing to risk not graduating. I lied and said I had not been drinking. I said the other guy may have been drinking, but I had nothing to do with that. I was unwavering in my story and felt no remorse. One of my teachers knew that I had been with the guy who got kicked out; she expressed disappointment in my not coming forward honestly. I told her she was crazy and that she was wrong to believe that I had been involved. The only thing that mattered to me was getting away with my misdeed.

The reality was I had been drinking and I got sick. I vomited in the back of a bus several times coming back from an outing in New York City. I stumbled into my dorm and passed out. I had gotten completely wasted to the point of partially blacking out on that excursion. I only vaguely recall drinking with two friends outside in a public square. I have no recollection of what occurred after the first few drinks. My next memories are being sick on the bus back to New Jersey.

This kind of situation would be repeated over and again for many years to come. From the beginning of college I drank alcohol basically anytime I could. I very soon started to layer in whatever other substances you put in front of me. Pot became a regular part of my life. I used poppers and opium as well. I ventured into ecstasy, cocaine, and Special K soon after. I discovered crystal meth in my third year of college.

Meth changed my life. It was exactly what I had been looking for. It made me feel powerful, sexy, and confident. Fortunately, I struggled to have a regular supply of it for a while. I attempted to deal ecstasy during my senior year, but I was too much of a junky to do it well. I ended up using too much of my own supply. I would sometimes get so messy that I would lose and/or have my supply stolen by others. Eventually, it just became too expensive to be a dealer, and I stumbled upon a new set of circumstances.

I spent the New Year of 2001 in New York City with some friends. We drove up in the midst of a blizzard. That weekend was a complete blur. That was typical for me, however. I spent the entire weekend consuming drugs and alcohol 24/7 with no sleep and very little food. I just stumbled from bars to clubs, from house to house.

On this trip, I met an older guy named Jake in the bathroom of the Roxy. It was New Year's Day and he invited me to go on to Twilo, a famous New York City nightclub, with him and his friends. He offered me free entrance and more drugs. I obliged because I had really wanted to see the club, but didn't have the money or anymore drugs. I don't recall much of that experience because I spent most of it in a K-hole, but I do recall feeling like I had arrived. I was at the best party in town, with all the coolest people, plus I'd gotten in for free. I had no money, my jeans were ripped from an earlier accident, and I had on a paper-thin jacket. The guy I met that night, Jake, described me as being a "hot mess." I cannot imagine what I looked like after three days of no sleep and not a sober breath.

Meeting Jake changed the direction of my life. I started going to New York City every weekend to visit him. Eventually he asked me to move in after I graduated. I had been planning to move to DC, because all my drug friends lived there. I realize now that I probably would have ended up dead or in jail had I moved to DC. I was most certainly part of the wrong crowd. Jake partied, but he was fifty-six and an established professional. He helped me to see the importance of keeping up appearances. But I was never able to successfully master the behaviors he modeled.

When I finally moved to New York City, I landed in Jake's four-story townhouse in the West Village. I had access to a convertible Mercedes and a beach house in Fire Island Pines. I was twenty-one going on twenty-two, and I truly had arrived. I was living the life that I had dreamed of. I went to circuit parties. I did drugs all the time. I had regular access to meth too. However, I was not happy with Jake. He was too old and I was not attracted to him. Yet, I stayed with him because I was afraid to leave the material things. I also felt sorry for him and did not want to hurt him. I threw myself harder into using in order to avoid facing these feelings. I had two hospitalizations from meth overdoses and I was fired from a job. I realized that I could not use meth safely, and stopped using it several times a week. I switched to an every-couple-of-months cycle, using mostly around holiday weekends.

I would still use on random weekends, particularly if I had been drinking too much and someone gave it to me. I felt like I was better able to control meth as time went on because I discovered benzodiazepines. I discovered that I could mitigate the paranoia and mania if I drank alcohol with two Ativan. I would use meth for a controlled amount of time and then when I was ready to return to "normal," I would sedate myself. I used meth like this for many years. Ultimately, meth contributed to my ending my relationship with Jake. I would not be able to bear his presence when I was coming off of meth. I would be filled with irritability, depression and anxiety for weeks after using meth. I was also drinking very heavily and taking ecstasy and Special K during this time.

My mental health was pretty fragile during this time, but I just assumed that was the way it goes as a gay party boy. Then I met a new guy, his name was Rick. He was only a few years older than I was and crazy handsome. I fell in love, or should I say I became obsessed with him? I left Jake and started dating Rick. To do this, I moved in with a friend and his girlfriend. I felt like I was about to get the perfect life I'd thought I was going to get when I came to New York. I could do things that people my age were doing, things I could not do when I was with Jake. I started going to happy hours and went out more regularly with peers. Alcohol became huge for me during this time, but the drugs still figured prominently. I was a regular at parties like Alegria.

I felt lost and hated my job in financial services. I thought going back to school would help me to change careers and find happiness. I applied to graduate school. Going back to school helped fill a partial void in my life— being busy and surrounded by intellectual people was good for me. My relationship with Rick was not good, though. We were not exactly compatible and the insecurity I felt with him pushed me to act out sexually. This was especially compounded when I used drugs and alcohol. Eventually, Rick dumped me because he caught me cheating.

I was devastated and became depressed and suicidal. I knew that my addictive personality was a big cause in my cheating. I started going to Sexual Compulsives Anonymous in my efforts to win Rick back. For the first time, it dawned on me that I might have a problem with drugs and alcohol, and I stopped using for about seventy days on my own. I also started sleeping with people in the rooms of S.C.A. and manipulated a married man to take me to Amsterdam with him. That trip hastened my drinking and using again. S.C.A. was not a good fit for me and eventually I stopped going. While it took me a long time to get over Rick, I started using the bars and clubs as means of moving forward. I did not spiral out again because being in school while working kept me sort of grounded. I still had moments of messiness, but over all I was too preoccupied to be a complete mess.

I dated a few guys here and there. I broke a few hearts. Eventually, I met a really nice guy from the gym. His name was Will, and he was nineteen years older than I was. He liked to drink and play video games. He also didn't seem to mind if I went out with my friends. It was a good fit. But a friend of mine who dabbled in coke offered me some and I quickly developed a love affair with it. Coke struck me as being more manageable and classier than meth. When I finished graduate school, I moved in with Will, but I had a lot of free time on my hands. I also no longer had to hold it together in order to survive on my own.

I was yet again safely nestled in a relationship with

someone who could take care of me. Secretly, I started seeking out my own supply of coke and was off to the races. During this time, my mother died from her addiction. Her liver failed and she could not stop using despite the warnings. I was not terribly close to my mother, yet her death derailed me inexplicably. My dabbling with coke turned into an every weekend and sometimes an everyday affair. I got drunk daily to mitigate the anxiety I was experiencing and as a counter balance to the coke. Whenever I got drunk, I wanted coke, so this made it challenging to not use daily.

Fortunately, my pocketbook did not lend itself to my using daily and I did care about my job—somewhat. But the weekends were definitely a time to cut loose. I became a complete and total cokehead. It was worse than meth because I was able to integrate coke into my daily life successfully. I could not function when I was on meth. It just completely turned me into a primordial creature that only wanted sex and more meth. Coke eventually did the same thing to me, but I found it easier to control at first.

I thought I was the hottest thing ever. I had a good paying job, a beautiful apartment, a dog, a boyfriend, Diesel jeans, and plates of coke. I drank lots of champagne and lived an active social life. I hit the bars and clubs with a vengeance. I felt I truly had arrived in a way that had eluded me previously. Inevitably, meth snuck back into my life. I would use meth when I wanted to get more bang for my buck or when people offered it to me. I noticed that meth did not seem to work for me the way that it had before. I probably needed to change the delivery mechanism, like smoking or injecting. Thankfully, I was too afraid to do either. Panic attacks were a constant battle for me, and I worried that I would end up back in the hospital if I used meth in a new way. I felt like I was in control of my drug usage during this time because I knew how to bring myself down when I needed to.

Eventually, I lost the ability to keep my drug usage neatly packaged into Fridays and Saturdays. It leaked into Mondays and Tuesdays. I was struggling with work. I was cheating on Will relentlessly. I was lying about everything. I was romantically obsessed with a married man. I was starting to have constant chest pains. I had lost fifteen pounds. I was just not in good shape. My outlook on life was pretty bleak. All I cared about was getting high and dealing with the consequences of my behavior. It dawned on me that I was not really living. I tried to stop using coke and meth, but I didn't consider giving up drinking. One or two drinks in and I was dialing or texting a dealer. I tried to put up blocks to using. I gave my wallet to Will, I would delete my dealer's number, I would give up my phone, and the list goes on. But I always found ways around all my efforts to not use. I recall feeling like I was not in control of my life. I was completely at the mercy of my disease. I contemplated killing myself often.

The last weekend I used was not particularly out of the ordinary for me. Yes, I had been drinking and drugging for six days straight. I had been going to work and functioning semi-normally, but I was still a raging mess. When the weekend rolled around, I was just using with impunity with no plan for stopping. I ended up calling in sick on a Monday so that I could keep getting high and hook up with guys online. On Monday night I called my dealer so that I could get high that night. I would not be going to work again on Tuesday. I went outside to retrieve a delivery of coke. On my way back inside, my dog started barking, which alerted Will to my having left the apartment. The dog's barking was so unusual because I had ventured in and out of the apartment all hours of the night for several years. I used to come and go all the time when I was using, either to get more drugs or to look for sex. I sometimes did not even come home until five or six a.m. There was never a peep from the dog, but for some reason this time—she went off.

Will came to me and asked what I was doing.

I said, "Nothing. Why?"

He asked what was in my hand.

I lied.

He then said he could not do this anymore.

For a split second I almost ended the relationship. But I suddenly had a moment of clarity and realized that I was willing to throw Will away over a bag of drugs. Three years with this guy and the white powder was more important. I said I was going to bed. I put the drugs in the Pyrex dish that I cut lines in and took two Ativan with a swig of wine.

I had no idea that was to be my last day using drugs.

I slept for the first time in two or three days. I recall feeling relieved that I was getting some sleep, and that I could get off the treadmill finally. I had not been able to stop, but I was so caught up in my addiction that I could not tell that I was not in control.

The next day I stayed home and rested all day. I spent some time looking into treatment options as well. Surfing the Web had never been more challenging. After all the countless hours looking for sex online, I suddenly could not make a simple Google search. Eventually, I found the name of an outpatient program. I wrote down the number, and I promised Will, and myself, that I would call the next day. I cooked a fierce dinner that night, with the requisite bottles of wine served. *Again, I had no idea that was to be my last drink.*

The next day I went back to work, a broken, tired wearisome shell of a person. I did call that outpatient program and spoke with an intake specialist. I made an appointment to come in the next day. I opted for outpatient because I was too embarrassed to go away for treatment. I did not consider A.A., because I did not think I was that kind of addict. In reality, I did not know anything about the program. I assumed that really broken people went there because they could not go anywhere else. I had not even heard of Cocaine Anonymous or Crystal Meth Anonymous.

When I went to intake at the outpatient, I remember feeling so defeated and lost. I could not believe that my life had become so tragic. Although that was the beginning of something amazing and profound, I could not look the counselor in the eyes. I felt dirty and ugly, yet I also felt like I was somehow better than all the people in the waiting room. I remember thinking how pathetic those other people looked and that I did not belong in that center.

I returned to outpatient the next day for a gay men's group. I did not love it at first, but by the end I felt like there was something there for me. I had to take a toxicology screen upon arrival and that added to the feeling that this was serious. I was told that people who relapse got sent to relapse prevention meetings at the center. If they continue to relapse, they are then sent to inpatient treatment. I did not want those outcomes, so I made a decision to not use. By the grace of some higher power, I became very ill that night after outpatient. I was feverish and weak. I considered picking up, but knew that it would not work. I get really overheated when I party, so it seemed like a bad idea to party while feverish. I just rested and found gratitude that I was able to stay clean for the first weekend in years. I remember thinking that I was going to wake up on Monday feeling rested and clear headed, a feeling that had eluded me for most of a decade. In retrospect, that first weekend was a freebie.

I emerged into my first full week of outpatient

treatment feeling a bit more secure and enthusiastic. I felt like I belonged in the outpatient program. In those early days, I wondered to myself how long I might stay in treatment and when I might return to some semblance of my party life. I had plans to go to Amsterdam for Gay Pride in August, so I was thinking that I might get back to normalcy then. For the time being, I decided to focus on what was in front of me, which was going to outpatient two-to-three evenings per week.

During this time, the working week was usually just fine, but as the weekend started to approach, I started to get uneasy. Fortunately, another freebie came my way. I went to Florida with Will to see his parents for a few days. In the past, I would have at least drunk profusely the entire time I was there, but generally I did not feel as a great a pull toward alcohol as I did toward coke and meth. It was a little odd ordering dinner and not having wine, but I got through that. Will joined me in solidarity and didn't drink either. His support helped me to not feel like I was missing out on something. I had a good several days in Florida, and I was grateful to get through another weekend still sober. I had not been able to cobble together two weekends clean since I was about eighteen years old.

I started to develop relationships with guys in my outpatient groups. This mattered greatly to me. Friendships were a huge part of why I dragged my feet about getting sober. I was afraid of not having any friends, since all my friends were party friends. It was great to meet guys trying to get sober. Supporting other guys helped me to stay clean. It felt awful when someone would relapse and leave the group. I committed to stay in my groups because I wanted to be there for the others. I also started venturing to other twelve-step meetings with guys from the group. We visited A.A. meetings, C.M.A. meetings, and C.A. meetings.

At first I was going just to be social. I had no desire to embrace the Twelve Steps, or to be a part of a fellowship. After auditing meetings for a month or two, I did start to hear things that resonated with me. In particular, I started going with guys from outpatient to a Friday night C.M.A. meeting. More than anything, I needed to be in the meeting so I could reprogram what Friday nights looked like for me. Friday usually involved me going shopping for an outfit, hitting the liquor store, calling my dealer, making plans for a bar or club later, and then getting trashed until sometime Sunday night.

It took me some time to reprogram myself, and I remember struggling a great deal on Friday nights. I would sometimes take a cab home from the meeting, and it would ride through parts of the city that I used to frequent. I would want to jump out the cab and go back to the way things were. Yet, wanting to remain clean for my outpatient brothers kept me on the path.

I had been a huge party boy. I went to all the big parties in New York City. Black Party weekend in March was huge. I had a little over two months clean when Black Party rolled around in 2010. I felt like everyone in the City was having fun except me. I was so miserable that weekend. I was shaking with anxiety and felt as if I would erupt at any moment. The physical urge to use was so intense that weekend. But I just kept thinking that if I held on until Monday, the desires would probably lift. I spent a great deal of time with Will and just kind of laid low. I had not yet discovered the magic of twelve-step meetings and I did not have an extensive contact list. Until that weekend, I did not understand the point of taking the phone numbers of other sober people when they were offered. I got through that weekend just barely. I now know I was truly lucky. Nonetheless, when I was headed to work on Monday morning, when I am sure I would have probably been blacked out at Alegria, I felt proud that I was doing something different. I later learned the term "sober reference." That Black Party weekend remains a powerful sober reference for me. I learned that I could be OK during significant events that would have involved my using drugs. I do not have to be drunk or high to have a good time. Being a gay man no longer had to be only about partying.

Eventually, just going to outpatient twice a week and auditing meetings stopped working. I started to feel crazy, and the desire to use returned. I sensed that I would not make it unless I started doing something more. I heard in meetings that getting a sponsor and doing the steps was helpful. I saw the evidence of this on the faces of many people in the rooms. I made a decision to give it a try, after years of ignoring the existence of the Twelve Steps. I started looking for a sponsor, and I went with the first person that hit on me. A guy named Joe came up to me in a meeting, and I could tell from the look in his eyes that he was looking for more than just being helpful. We agreed to meet for dinner one night to discuss working together. Fortunately, I did not find him terribly attractive, but I liked the attention. Old habits die hard, I suppose. I did not understand anything he said to me during our meeting. I left feeling confused and frustrated about the whole process, but I kept reaching out to him and going to meetings a few times a week.

That May, I garnered another powerful sober reference. I was invited to go to Washington, DC for a DJ contest. DC is like ground zero for me. My first hospitalization resulted from a drug-fueled weekend in DC. Everyone I knew there was a drug addict or dealer. All my previous memories of DC involved going from clubs to after hours at people's homes. I never actually saw the city. The last time I had been in DC, which was

October 2009, I was D.J. at an after-hours party. I was up for two days and consumed massive amounts of drugs. I lost my cell phone and could not drive back home. I was entirely too frazzled, despite being the person who drove down to DC. I had to ask Will to drive us back. All I could do is curl up in the back seat and nurse an alcoholic beverage and take Ativan. I was a sketchy mess. So, it was no small feat that I was returning to DC for a DJ contest on a Saturday afternoon.

I talked about the trip with my outpatient group, and they told me not to go. I was not willing to cancel the trip, so I agreed to take someone with me and to only go for one day. I asked Will to take the train down with me. We got a hotel and booked our return train early Sunday morning. I made no plans to meet up with friends after the contest. Instead, Will and I made plans to have a nice dinner and get to bed early, exactly as my counselor had suggested.

Admittedly, I was completely miserable. I saw many of the people I used with and had been invited out to a party on Saturday night. I knew that I could not go. I would have immediately asked for a hit of something and then been off to the races. Will said he would leave me in DC if I ended up picking up. He had no desire to be caught in one of my runs. I was happy to return to New York on Sunday morning. My friends in DC were less than thrilled. Later, I realized that my journey into sobriety in many respects became a question of me staying alive versus me staying relevant to people I called friends. The ones that are meant to be a part of my life today still are; those that were not meant to be a part of my life are gone.

Around the time that I had six months clean and sober, I was faced with an interesting challenge. Will and I had planned to go away with our party friends for Will's fiftieth birthday. We had planned this over a year ago—

before I was in sobriety. We planned to go to Amsterdam for Pride and then off to Prague for a week. When I started my sober journey in February, I had in my mind that I would go back to my old ways once this trip rolled around. I had just wanted to feel better. It was not my intention to stay clean permanently. I assumed that I could party manageably once I had settled down. Yet a voice said to me that I probably could not go back to the old ways without risking being stuck in the old ways. The folks in my outpatient hammered this point into me during the weeks leading up to the trip. My new sponsor said I should not go, either. But, he understood that the plans had been made with other people long ago. Obviously, the wisest decision would have been to not go at all, because Amsterdam is a drug-filled city, where I had partied hard before. But I went and it was crazy hard.

I had decided that I wanted to stay sober. This of course was a disappointment to most of my travel companions. Will was supportive for the most part. I was sad that I could not trip on 'shrooms, though. I had a fun and illuminating experience on 'shrooms the last time I was in Amsterdam for Gay Pride. But I had a made a commitment to my outpatient group and my sponsor.

To get through the trip, I emailed my sponsor every day. I went to a meeting in Amsterdam. Fortunately, it was rainy and cold most of the time we were there and being out in the streets among the outdoor parties did not appeal as much. God works in mysterious ways. I was also lucky that we had only planned to be in Amsterdam for a weekend, and left for Prague on Monday morning. We parted ways with some of the more challenging folks on the trip. The smaller group that went to Prague was tamer, even though two of those people had been among my hardcore club and using friends. Still, I made it through the trip without a drink or a drug. I returned to New York and my outpatient program feeling relieved that the trip was over. I had some fun, but it was really hard being with that group of people under those circumstances.

I got my first service commitment at an A.A. meeting during my first six months. Today, I do service in A.A. and C.M.A., but earlier on I felt more comfortable in A.A. meetings. In particular, I felt more at ease in meetings where there was a mix of men and women, and A.A. offered more of that. My first service position was literature chair for a meeting, which terrified me. I had gone to the monthly business meeting to nominate another friend for the position. He wanted it, but he got nominated for another commitment. By default, I wound up accepting the position, and it turned out to be a good thing.

I had so much fear and anxiety around that meeting. I felt like no one liked me and people were unfriendly. Ironically, that group is one of my home groups today. I feel completely at ease there and the people love me. Funny how my perception can be so totally off! That first service commitment saved my life. It helped me during Gay Pride, my birthday, the Europe trip and other points over the six months I had the position. I did not want to have to come back to the group and tell them I had relapsed and therefore needed to give up the position. I also had to make an announcement at each meeting and that helped people learn my name and face. It took over a year for me to feel at ease in that meeting, but getting involved really helped me to not run away. I was so uncomfortable that without something rooting me to that meeting, I am sure I would have run away. I like to run away, but sobriety has taught me to stand and face my fears.

It dawned on me one day that I had to keep going no matter what. I did not want to relapse, so I started going to the meetings on my own. Making that decision was crucial for the sobriety I have today. In short order, I realized I did not need to rely upon any one person. I could find the support I needed among the collective "Fellowship" of the rooms. The fears and reservations I had about people not liking me started to melt away. All it took was making an effort to connect with others and being open minded. It helped that I had continued to work the steps with my sponsor. I do not think I did the steps perfectly, but I do not believe I needed to. I only need to do the first step perfectly.

I found myself immersed in meetings, connected to a wider array of people, and within striking distance of a year clean. Wanting to make a year became a strong guiding force that propelled me through my first sober New Year's Eve. Celebrating the New Year had always been a major party event for me. I had to at least make it to a year, but that meant making it through New Year's Eve. It felt like an important goal to attain, since people talked about it so much in recovery. A group of loving and supportive friends, along with a diner full of people I did not know, showed me love. At midnight they sang happy anniversary, and I gave a speech.

I sort of always believed that I could reach a year. Yet, there were definitely times when staying sober did not seem that important to me. I do not know how or why I stayed sober. I still cannot explain why I am still here, nearly three years later. I guess it has something to do with what I was taught in the rooms. Don't pick up no matter what. Help other people and take the focus off of me. Learn to rely on a power greater than me. I did those things early on, even though I did not understand what I was doing. I continue to do these things in ever evolving ways. The connection I have with my Higher Power is not the same as it was in the early days. I have so much more faith and evidence that this program works.

When I was in early sobriety, a friend suggested I read *The Sermon on the Mount* by Emmett Fox. I happened to be going through one of my self-help phases, so it made sense. I also was attending meetings for a group that closed with the "Lord's Prayer." *The Sermon on the Mount* dissects the "Lord's Prayer" in painstaking detail. I found the book to be both illuminating and it helped to shape my concept of a higher power. *The Sermon on the Mount* taught me that my primary purpose is to be useful to others. God's will for me is to be of service and help another human being. Upon reading that, I no longer felt lost in the world. It had always been somewhat easy for me to be nice to people or to bestow random acts of kindness upon others. Yet I always did things in the hopes that people would like me or that they would praise me in some way. I am not entirely cured of those desires, but mostly I just help people because it is the right thing to do.

I believe that kindness comes back to me, usually not from the person that I was kind to, particularly if that person is a stranger. By and large I just try to live my life to be helpful and useful. The benefit to me is I get to spend that moment not thinking about myself. That brings me immense freedom and serenity. It is painful and tiring to only think about myself. Too much time thinking about me leads me to negative and fear based thoughts. I have found a design for living that has vastly improved my life circumstances. I no longer live life only thinking about what I can get from everyone else. I try to live life thinking about what I can give to everyone else. I learned this from Emmett Fox's book, but the same principles have been reinforced in twelve-step fellowships. I have read other books that discuss the path to happiness, and they all agree that helping others is the key. I have held onto this. I believe that I could probably follow this formula without being in a twelve-step program, but I choose to stay because I would rather not do this alone. I am less effective when I do things on my own.

I stay in twelve-step fellowships because I enjoy being connected to so many like-minded people who are on a path to a better way of being. I model behavior after people who I see are in a better place than me. For too long, I unknowingly did the opposite. I modeled my behavior after people who were traveling a destructive path, but those paths seemed cooler than mine. I had no idea when I set out to get clean that I would decide to keep showing up.

I also had no idea that twelve-step recovery would turn out to be a spiritual program designed to help us rely on power greater than ourselves. I was shocked the first time someone asked me in my outpatient if I ever prayed. I was, like, "What does that have to do with any of this?"

The fact is, I had dabbled in prayer for as far back I can remember, but mostly I prayed for superficial things. My grandmother and grandfather had suggested I pray when I was a kid. I was taught a very rudimentary prayer when I was a kid, but it was a very sophomoric prayer. I did not receive any further education on prayer or on spirituality. I mostly grew up thinking church was stupid and that overly religious people were to be avoided. I pretty much relied on my own powers to get me through or so I thought.

I know now that God has been with me all the time. I just was not consciously connected to him in a meaningful way until I got into recovery. Being in recovery has taught me the importance of asking for help from my HP. I have also learned the importance of acknowledging the answers and help I receive. I did always believe that something had to be watching over me because I managed to get out of many scrapes and situations without serious harm. Overwhelmingly, I discredited God and thought that my cleverness was the path to success and happiness. I must say, my life has gotten so much easier and more manageable since I have learned to rely on a power greater than me.

My concept of God or a higher power is a fluid one. Sometimes it is a more traditional God figure that I think is a male, father-like being. Sometimes it is simply the Universe. Sometimes it is just a power greater than myself like the twelve-step meeting rooms or the fellowships that I am a member of. It no longer matters to me what my higher power is. I just have to believe that there is something greater than me.

It is easy for me to see the ways A.A. or C.M.A. are greater than I am, which helps to reinforce my faith and reliance. I can without a doubt see the greatness in those fellowships. I see people changing and growing every day. I hear people say that living in sobriety is hard. I am not sure I know what they mean. In fact, people say life is hard. I do not agree with that as a blanket statement. Yes, there are terribly challenging periods in my life. There have been times when I did not think I would make it, even in sobriety. Although I do not think those periods define the entirety of my experience.

Overwhelmingly, I think life is an adventure that challenges me to grow. My path is such that I do not ever get bored, and I am continually forced to accept the impermanence of life. I have rich experiences and I make mistakes all the time, but I am fortunate enough to see them as opportunities to change and learn. There is a part of me that likes the safety of things staying the same all the time. When things get good, I want more and more of the good. Yet, I know that is not possible and it is far more constructive for me to focus on moving forward through good and bad. My goal is to be OK no matter what life throws at me. Twelve-step recovery has offered me a set of tools to work toward that goal. It is an imperfect practice, but I am content to continue along this journey. I cannot imagine being mired in active addiction again. I respect that it is a real possibility for someone like me, but for now I am willing to do what is necessary to stay sober. I leave the future to my Higher Power.

Diamonds and the Rough
R. J. Hughes

Everyone was so handsome.

At my first gay A.A. meeting, a few days out of rehab, still cloudy from those tempestuous dreary decades of alcoholic deluge, I saw beauty in the faces of the sober men at Lambda.

Lambda, on the Upper West Side of Manhattan, used to be called a "husband-hunters" meeting, as so many of the alcoholics who frequented it were there to meet potential partners in sobriety. Not a sober way of thinking, by the way (you're not in A.A. to find a date, but to discover and maybe accept yourself), but a normal one. Especially if you've lived a large part of your life sequestered from society of any sort, except for the delivery boy who dropped off the bottles you'd ordered for the "party" you were throwing for dozens of imaginary friends.

To someone newly in recovery, anyone who's had a good night's sleep can seem the picture of sobriety. To me, whose body had just begun to heal, whose mind had begun to awaken, the men at Lambda were paragons of health, happiness, liberty, awareness. I saw them not as flawed men who'd struggled to make something of their tattered lives but as saviors who would rescue me from the chasm of loneliness into which I'd hurled myself.

I wanted to connect with them. I wanted to be held. I wanted to feel.

I wanted to be hurt.

And so, naturally, I fell in love with everyone who said hello. It seemed like love, but was actually confusion masquerading as desire for someone who was wrong for me. At another point this would not have seemed so fraught with implications for future misery, but at the time every moment of interaction with another man was perilous: The pursuit of happiness through miscomprehension.

I mistook courtesy for romantic interest, friendliness for affection. I saw in the clear eyes of everyone around me not the simple directness I would later come to recognize as a part of sobriety, but a come-on. I was so desperate for connection that I lacked discrimination.

And so everyone was handsome.

This didn't last long. People didn't turn ugly, but they began slowly to appear human rather than godlike. As I adapted to a world of sun and light and air and emotion I began to see people more for what they were than for what I'd hoped they would be to me.

This awakening first began to surface through sport. Softball. Somehow, one of us had had the idea that fifteen to twenty gay men would enjoy playing ball. It wasn't me, I was too fresh from the clink to think much about anything other than the wonder of it all. But I was invited to join this ad hoc light-in-the-loafers athlete's collective, and so, for eight or ten late Saturday mornings in the spring and summer of the first year of my sobriety, it was play ball. I retrieved my Little League mitt from an old valise and joined several gay men in recovery and traipsed uptown to a field along Riverside Park, with a gleaming view of the lordly Hudson, the humming West Side Highway, the patchy meadows dappled by sycamore trees alongside us fronting the concrete arches of the Amtrak tunnel. Bucolic and urban and blessedly off the beaten path.

Few of us played well. I was a decent pitcher, though a hopeless batter, but we were in the open air. We were spending honest time together (not that we knew it then). We weren't cruising, or pining, or sighing regrets. We weren't haunting dreary bars that reeked of disinfectant and stale music or longing for the unattainable (unless an unlikely homerun not based on a fielding error counted). We were discovering, without knowing it, how to relate to each other in new ways. Not through deep conversation (I had no idea what that might entail then), not through romance, not even through innuendo and quoted movie dialogue, but through the simple act of being together.

The softball games were, as you might expect, a mixed bag of masculine and not-so-masculine attributes, of athleticism and awkward acrobatics. Sissies mincing up the baseline giggling at their ineptitude. Butch guys pretending they knew more about batting and fielding than they probably did. Regular guys who were so effortlessly masculine they could have been straight. Helpless loners ashamed of themselves for what they thought they'd remembered and grateful for the company of people who never knew them when.

No one would mistake us for anything other than a bunch of somewhat suspect guys tossing a ball around. Being mistaken for someone suspect no longer mattered as much as it had. Little by little I had begun to shake off my fear of being compromised by associating with either alcoholics or gay men in uncompromising daylight.

Unlike a younger generation that seems to be more at ease with gayness, I was forty at the time of my last drink, and had been one of those tiresome homosexuals who needed to get drunk to engage with another man, if engagement meant throwing caution to the windand accepting the clammy embrace of someone as desperate as I was for guilty sex.

It wasn't actually the sex that was guilty, though. It wasn't even the desire. I was fine with all of that. It was something beyond physicality that I hungered for and feared. It was being known. Iwanted somehow to be understood without having to open myself up, without having to share even the smallest mortified piece of whatever I was.

It was something beyond the physicality that I hungered for and feared. It was a mental state of terror. It was the being known. I never wanted to be known. Simply, maybe, understood without explanation. Or even admired for my mystery. Oblivion allowed me to let my guard down and pretend to be available.

My emotions were made of illusions, and my illusions were made of resentments. Nothing as real as feeling, only the stubborn sensation of missed opportunity, of envy, and the sad realization that the word that defined my behavior best was "squander."

But with the trepidation of early recovery, and the whisper of hope that followed an actual night of sleep so profound my rehab roommate had thought I was dead, I began to think that if I tried to *be* rather than to *yearn*, that I might arrive at something approaching whatever it was that I wasn't then. At least something that wasn't a sad-sack who'd squandered his gifts.

At my rehab, the curiously named Rhinebeck Lodge for Successful Living (like something Ayn Rand might have dreamt of, had a stay there been a guarantee of wads of money and unmatched personal aggrandizement), I'd had an actual revelation. There among the snowy trees of upstate New York during the bleak tail end of an unbending winter when the longer afternoons began to return, I slowly accepted my fate. I was someone who needed help. Or at least someone who needed to ask for help, which made all the difference.

But the real revelation came when two men arrived to speak to our group. We were a dozen or so, the usual lineup: a teen heroin addict, an angry husband there to shut his wife up about his drinking, a regretful housewife who'd gulped painkillers while her children managed to break the locks on the baby-proof outlets, a Long Island stoner and ex-surfer with a remarkable sun-cured forehead that gleamed like fresh pemmican, an unhappy rosy-cheeked cop terrified of having to face his beer-guzzling fellow officers when he returned to the precinct. And me, the sensitive soul who'd preferred to read the vodka-soaked exploits of the Brothers Karamazov to spending time chatting with the other patients.

These two visiting men, former Rhinebeck Lodge residents whose names were forgotten to me as soon as they'd uttered them, told us their stories, their messy drunkalogues, their tales of misery and that hackneyed thing called redemption we've all come to expect from three-act movie scripts. I don't recall the specifics of what they said, but for the honesty with which they said it (though the middle-aged surfer with the deer-jerky face later told me he was sure they had made everything up). What struck me was how, when they weren't addressing us, when they spoke quietly to each other afterward, transparency glistened in the air between them. No secrets. No subterfuge. No manipulation for the sake of manipulating. It was kindness, even tenderness, between two men who wanted nothing from each other, but who offered much. It was dignity. It was respect.

Rehab is a way station, of course. A palace of babies. I spent my early nights there observing the moon blotches on the wall and trying not to make harsh torment of the solitude as I'd used to. By the fourth or fifth day, I'd begun to disassemble the despair of my decades past, and consider the possibility of bliss beyond the mutes of the plaster walls.

I took that image of the two men with me when I left rehab a week or so later, and began to make my way in a clearer world. Playing softball with Bruce and Jose and Kyle and Steve gave me a start at socializing, the chance to be where I began, a curious seeker of unresolved music.

Alcoholism is a leveler. Any addiction is. My recovery started out egalitarian, but I quickly began to notice who among the others in recovery were most responsive to this new life. I began to notice the blue buildings in the summer air, the hesitation of wind upon the rustling day. I began to feel the gradations of heat and cold. I began to see the men I'd met as mortal, not saviors, not angels of mercy, but fellows who spoke to me as if I were there to be spoken to, not negotiated with. I began to carve out acquaintances.

This was new to me. Camaraderie. Even ease among others. I had been so blind to the drunken behaviors I'd exhibited, had become in the tender mornings of my early recovery sensitive to the light of other eyes that this tossing back-and-forth of a softball, this swinging and missing, was a way to be foolish, to learn to accept foolishness in myself. We were all so serious, and I more serious than anyone, because I was someone who despite the indignities of a life badly lived had considered himself still too worthy of the chorus to traffic with the faceless crowd. Too noble to be mocked.

But on the softball field I was mocked, and I was laughed at, and I was the object of kind derision for my pretensions and my lingering arrogance. In the fullness of the season, when spring succumbed to summer, I started to slough off my priggish self-importance. I began to appreciate things for what they were rather than what I wished them to be.

And everyone was handsome. Even if they weren't good-looking, they were real. I began to speak with transparency, with respect, with regard, with the realization that the moment was the moment and nothing more, for all I had was that brief connection and, in a life of squandering, I no longer wanted to squander the numinous opportunity to look into the eyes of someone else and, even without truly knowing him – or me – be present for him. That counted more than my fantasy of rescue or romance. I had begun to want what I had just begun to discover: humility.

We Try to Grow
Mike C.

I'm fairly certain the first time I ever masturbated was the same day I first got drunk. Memory plays its tricks, but that's my recollection. As far back as I can bring to mind, sex and alcohol were inextricably intertwined. But what I can remember is that it was in the afternoon and I was alone upstairs. I recall a fumbling, repetitive motion that suddenly took on an urgency of its own and this twelve-year-old boy had his first orgasm and first ejaculation. I was astounded. It was like a bike ride down a steep hill with no brakes, a scary and joyful loss of control.

My first drunk was at a wedding that evening. The bride's brothers—at ages eighteen and nineteen—were almost grown-up. They said knowingly, "There's *vodka* in the punch!"

I wasn't quite sure what that was, but I quoted them over and over all night. As the adults laughed at me, I was getting tipsy. I was a chubby boy with glasses, cute enough and funny, and already I felt like a misfit. I envied my brother, a year older, who was tall, thin, good-looking, and knew how to talk to girls. With the vodka, however, I suddenly became handsome and popular too, or so it seemed.

It was a Ukrainian family wedding, with lots of polkas

and waltzes. I had no idea how to waltz or polka. Fueled by vodka, and a post-orgasm glow, it seemed to me that I could do anything! I was everything I wanted to be and the center of attention. Just before we left, my brother had kissed a girl. Even with the vodka, I wasn't *quite* brave enough for that. Maybe, I thought, with enough vodka, I would be the next time.

I didn't really *want* to kiss a girl; I just knew that I *should* want to. Raised with heterosexuality the norm, I knew this long before I wanted to kiss anyone at all. Then puberty arrived and made sense of all my feelings of not fitting in, of being different. I wanted to be with older boys, with men; I lusted after them in a thousand ways. Frightened by my feelings, I hid. I was a good kid, an excellent student, if non-athletic (Showers with guys? No way!), never any trouble. To the surprise of my vaguely Protestant family, I fled to the security of fundamental Christianity in my junior high years, a church that drew a sharp line between right and wrong, and promised deliverance from my problems.

In high school, some of the neighbor guys I'd grown up with would cut class to smoke and get high. Marijuana was actually easier to come by for us than booze. I'd hang out with them, but I never touched any of this stuff. Never smoked a joint or even a cigarette. I had a sense that if I ever let my barriers fall, they would fall down completely. Drugs, after all, were illegal. And cigarettes, although grown-up, were poisonous. But alcohol? Drinking was sophisticated, it was champagne on New Year's Eve.

Drinking, it seemed to me, was like sex: one of those great things grown-ups got to do. Like having a job, spending money, driving a car: activities reserved for adults. I loved watching old black and white movies on late night television. I wanted to be Katharine Hepburn sharing cocktails with Cary Grant, Lauren Bacall with

Humphrey Bogart in a swank nightclub. So, despite going to church and being a good and fearful kid, a few times in high school I did end up drinking.

With drinking came loosened inhibitions and the possibility of sex. I thought if *I* got drunk and my older brother's friend *Tom* got drunk and we both ended up in my bed, *something* might happen. There were a few times like that. Whether it was too much hiding or not enough alcohol, though, nothing ever did.

During the spring of my senior year, I traveled across the country for the first time to visit colleges I'd applied to. The age for drinking, which was twenty-one in Oregon where I grew up, was only eighteen then in New York. At Columbia, my hosts (straight juniors, so sexy and untouchable) took me to a (straight) nightclub in Greenwich Village, with pizza, a well-known folk singer, blue swirls of cigarette smoke, and my first legal beer. On that same outing, I hold a memory as clear as yesterday: a man stopped on the street to cruise me. *This* was the big city, and I knew I had to live there.

At the first college mixer I got drunk enough to knock over a wine bottle and then hit on a cute blond guy from Boston. A couple of weeks later the two of us got drunk enough at a club downtown to admit we might both be "bisexual." The next weekend found us screwing up our courage to enter a gay bar on West 10th Street. A man bought me drinks and asked me for my number. I had sex for the first time, I came out, and I dated. By mid-semester that fall, I was cutting class to spend a Friday afternoon in that bar, sharing my romantic trials with the bartender over beer and a burger. I felt grown-up, alive, and completely at home.

Fast-forward twelve years; alcohol and sex went from being new and magical to constant, demonic, and compulsive. It didn't happen all at once, though, and I didn't see it happening. I can't tell when drinking went from something I wanted to do, to something I needed to do. I can't pinpoint exactly when sex went from dreams of love and romance to a driven ugliness, a desperate need that left me lonelier than ever. Constantly going out, drinking, cruising, picking up, being picked up, acting out, passing out.

Drugs came in somewhere along the way, even as I told myself they weren't really my thing. After all, they were illegal. Scary. Drinking was something everyone did. Drinking was something it was OK to do. I just needed to get it under control. And love—I just needed to find true love, to get the sex under control, to find the right guy, or the right drinks, the right combination of drugs, to get everything under control.

I had no intention of quitting drinking, well, maybe temporarily. To get it under control. But my life was *way* out of control, and the sex was *completely* out of control, unsafe, and scary, and the drugs were … well, there were too many drugs, really, and they were scary, too. Money, friends, my job, the rent on my sublet—everything was getting out of control. In a moment of clarity, my problems seemed to me like a set of Russian nesting dolls. There was the big problem with compulsive sex. Open that doll up; the little doll inside told me it seemed to only happen when I did coke. Open that doll up—I only did coke when I drank. Open that one up—I drank nearly every day, always more than I intended too, leaving me broke and despondent. OK, I thought, I'll start there. *Try to get the drinking under control, first.*

I came to A.A. because my friend Bob was going to meetings. So a gay man took me to a gay and lesbian group for my first meeting (not in Manhattan, but Morristown, New Jersey). I had no prior personal knowledge of A.A., no real idea of what to expect.

I pictured it sort of like the Red Cross, we'd meet in church basements, almost refugees, and people would put a warm cup of coffee into my shaking hands. Well, there *was* coffee. What I found instead was a nice library upstairs at an Episcopal rectory, some cute Jersey boys, and lots of laughter. Afterwards, Bob and I talked late into the night, first in a diner and then back at my tiny studio. I found out he'd been hiding some pretty deep shit from me—surprise, the same stuff I was keeping from him: indiscriminate drug use, promiscuity, unsafe sex. So on first entering A.A. as a thirty- year-old gay man in Manhattan, I had little problem identifying with what I heard.

As I began going to meetings, I worried that A.A. was just another conversion experience. Like the one I'd known as a teen, getting "born again" so I wouldn't be gay. Even as I stayed clean and sober, I was scared that it would be only temporary. From the first night I walked in, I hadn't had a drink or a drug; how long could that last? In the rooms, I was apprehensive when I heard echoes of Christian fundamentalism. The nickname "The Big Book" sounded almost biblical, and people quoted it with reverence, as if it were scripture that settled all issues. It sometimes read like scripture too. "Having had a spiritual awakening" (*Alcoholics Anonymous*, 60), "We were reborn" (*A.A.*, 63).

In my teenage years, the emotional experience of being "born again" hadn't provided a permanent answer to my problems. I didn't see how it could now. I did not want to "convert" to Alcoholics Anonymous. The most common expression I heard for it was "the Program," which sure sounded like a cult. People talked about the "suggested" steps, yet some members were pretty dogmatic about them, and that concerned me.

In my first few weeks, attending meetings, I listened

avidly but I took it all in provisionally, trying to reserve judgment. Among the many suggestions, "get a sponsor" grated the most. It made it sound like a lodge's initiation ceremony. And I heard it at every meeting. Groups made announcements that they had a list of "temporary" sponsors available for "newcomers." More brainwashing, I thought.

Eating at a coffee shop after one meeting, I bitched about this to my new friends. One of them, Bill, a man nearing sixty, who looked like a leprechaun, said, "Well, you can take my number and tell people *I'm* your temporary sponsor, if it bothers you that much."

I said I would take him up on that, and by the way, would he mind if I called him? Not a problem, he said. He gently offered me help, not dogma.

Along with being afraid that A.A.'s cure would only be temporary, I also feared that with my sordid mix of troubles A.A. would reject *me*. I remember sitting down a few days later with Bill. He claimed continuous sobriety for twenty-seven years; I had a little trouble believing this. I told him my recent history of men, sex, drugs, and alcohol; problems with money and debt, failures in love, troubled relations with friends and family; fears at work and with life in general. I fully expected Bill to say that A.A. really couldn't help me; that my issues were too complicated. Instead, he looked straight at me and said, "You sound like just another drunk." I felt an immense relief; I was one *of* and not separate *from*.

A.A. didn't reject me; the fellowship accepted me as a whole, with all my problems. I got sober in urban and sophisticated Manhattan, with a gay meeting as my home group; but in my experience this acceptance can be found in A.A. everywhere. I've been going to meetings off-and-on for more than twenty-three years now. I can tally up meetings in at least twenty states, three provinces, and five foreign countries. Lots of meetings weren't in big cities. Often enough, I've been the only gay person in the room, as far as I can tell. Yet only a handful of times have I've sensed that my open sharing is surprising anyone, earning a cold shoulder or a disapproving glance. I've felt far worse in the world outside than within A.A. Perhaps that's because to stay sober, we are trying "to practice these principles in all our affairs" (*A.A.*, 60). One of these primary principles is open-mindedness. Besides, as I learned early on from a loud and unmistakable dyke: "I've never been to a straight meeting! How can it be a straight meeting if *I'm* there?"

Every October, the Bill W. Dinner Dance is an annual fundraiser for New York City's Intergroup. It is named after the founder of A.A. and it fills the largest hotel ballroom in Manhattan with hundreds of sober men and women from all walks of life. This event proves out that in A.A., "We are people who normally would not mix" (*A.A.*, 17).

The first time I went, I said hello to friends who were people I wouldn't have known a year earlier. I remember a policeman from Queens, a postman and his wife from Brooklyn, a doorman, a union leader, an Episcopal priest. The women were dressed like it was the prom, with hair up and makeup on; the men were mostly in their best suits. The room was full with noise and color. This fundraiser was not an inexpensive evening; in my early sobriety, being able to afford it was a point of pride. My sponsor and his best friend had gathered eight other gay men for our table. Other tables were filled with faces I knew from meetings, some straight and some gay. My sponsor, with his twenty-seven years in the Program, recognized people from all over town, and we shook hands and chatted around the room. After the dinner and the speakers, there was dancing, slow with Big Band music in the ballroom, and disco upstairs.

At this time, I worked in sales, frequently attending company conferences with dancing. There, I'd dance with my female co-workers or colleagues. I would never have danced with a man. Not with the other gay men I knew, even though we were out to each other and to everyone else. In a room full of people who knew I was gay, I would have been uncomfortable dancing with another gay man. If I had, it would have been taken as a political statement, maybe caused some snide remarks.

Yet that night at the Bill W. Dinner, when the dancing started, it never occurred to me *not* to ask the guy I'd been flirting with all evening to dance. He said yes, and I danced with him, and with gay friends from other groups, all so handsome in their tuxedos. Surrounded by hundreds of strangers, I didn't sense any disapproval or much surprise. My sponsor told me later that even before Stonewall same-sex couples danced together at the Bill W. Dinner and the straight A.A. members there took it in stride. I don't think it was just because we were in Manhattan, either. In A.A., "love and tolerance of others is our code" (*A.A.*, 84).

Perhaps, because I expected that tolerance, it became what I experienced—then and in many times and places since. I have warm and special memories from those Bill W. Dinner dances in my first few years; dressed up and hoping I looked my best, enjoying an evening of fellowship, close friendship, even romance.

I let go of my fears that A.A. was a cult, or a temporary conversion. I saw from my friends around me that a spiritual awakening could be a process of growth and change rather than a single, transformative moment. "Reborn" was after all only a metaphor. My sponsor's decades of sobriety made me think that a gay man could enjoy a long, satisfying life without constant nights out in gay bars and recreational drugs every weekend. With new sober friends, meetings, and activities, gay A.A. in Manhattan became a comfortable cocoon: a warm, safe, and temporary shelter, a place to change.

Could I be sober and continue to go to gay bars? That was a prickly and divisive question when I started attending meetings, especially before the Internet created new opportunities for hooking up. I heard a variety of opinions, mostly a variation on "hang out in a barbershop long enough and you'll end up with a haircut." At the time, I was sick of bars and the way I'd behaved in them, so instead I hung out in coffee shops after meetings with other sober gay men. Different gay A.A. groups put on dances and parties that sometimes felt like high school all over again, sometimes even holding them in high schools, yet now in a good way. I learned I could laugh and flirt with a soda in my hand instead of a drink. I found new places to socialize where alcohol wasn't a priority: more dances at our community center, working out at the gym.

Over time, I have lived and traveled to many other places, and often going to a gay bar was a quick and easy way to meet men for friendship, not just for romance or sex. Now I live in Seattle, and one of my closest A.A. friends would never miss the Friday country-western nights at the Cuff; another is a Sunday regular at Re-bar for house music. I have no problem going to a bar, not drinking, and having a great time. The advice I heard when I started was great then, and it's still what I would tell a newbie. If I have a good reason (other than drinking) to go to a bar, go and enjoy myself. If I am going there to get pleasure from being around drinking, find something else to do.

Sobriety has been no guarantee of morality. I can behave just as badly without a drink as with one. I've gone to meetings and treated them like a night out in a bar: checking out the crowd and cruising, paying no attention to anything being said. As much as I felt that A.A. accepted all of me, and all my problems, getting sober was not a panacea. It acted more like a sharp knife cutting through a knotted tangle of strings. Being alcohol and drug free allowed me to begin working on other issues; in and of itself, it didn't solve them.

Many times in a meeting, I've heard something like "After all, I'm just an alcoholic!" or "Well, that's alcoholism!" as if this addiction explained everything, every mistake I made. Just as often as I've heard the phrase an "alcoholic mind." I don't know what that is. Looking at my own life when I came to A.A., my alcohol abuse compounded my problems with money, sex, and much else. If there is something that can be labeled an alcoholic personality, I surely have it. However, I don't find that concept useful, maybe because it feels like its avoiding personal responsibility. It was important at first to identify, to feel that I was "just an alcoholic!" but wallowing in that mindset doesn't fix anything.

"Addiction is addiction, it's all the same," that's another opinion I've questioned. "It's just switching deck chairs on the *Titanic*." How does that explain my smoking? After all, I've learned everything I needed to know about relapse and denial from cigarettes: lying, hiding, using again, and quitting over and over. Having one puff at a party, or after work, after *years* without a smoke, and next thing desperately buying a fresh pack, chain-smoking. Without a doubt, I'm chemically addicted to nicotine, and it's an addiction that feels fresh and ever-present. Within A.A., however, I see every other possible variation of responses to nicotine. Some members quit easily while still drinking; some never smoked; some are smoking after decades sober, and they don't consider it an issue; some stay smoke-free without a hitch, yet are constantly relapsing with alcohol.

So I feel that addiction's not always just addiction; the difference in the substance or behavior does matter. For me, gambling does nothing. I have some food and spending issues but they are hardly life-destroying. On the other hand, I think if I tried crystal meth, even once, I might never stop. For me, it isn't worth the risk.

With alcohol, drugs, and nicotine, my safe intake level is "none." A therapist who was not in A.A. once told me that lifetime abstinence from alcohol was not a sustainable model. Well, for me it's worked so far, and seems as reasonable as living without nicotine, cocaine, or crystal meth.

"Now, about sex. Many of us needed an overhauling there" (*A.A.*, 68). Even if sex was an addiction, abstinence was not a sustainable or healthy alternative. I've spent a lifetime erasing childhood voices that said being gay, or sexuality itself, was bad. A.A. did not ask me to give up sex or my gay identity. What I did hear suggested was that (being single) I take a break from dating and new sexual relations for my first ninety days. That was a suggestion I heard for all newcomers, not just gay men. I fell into a temporary celibacy in early sobriety, but I wasn't following rules; it just came naturally, a welcome break after the previous strenuous activity. Soon enough that vacation was over and I needed to look at my sexual compulsivity; define what health meant in a sexual context, being gay and single in Manhattan at thirty-one.

I found that A.A. gave me the freedom to make my own choices about sex. In fact, making such choices was a strong suggestion found in the Big Book. "We tried to shape a sane and sound ideal for our future sex life. We subjected each relation to this test—was it selfish or not? We asked God to mold our ideals . . . whatever our ideal turns out to be" (*A.A.*, 69).

Whatever my ideal is—this was and is an incredibly

liberating passage. I am impressed that it was written in the '30s, when the prevailing morality was very different. The authors could have written something safer, more limiting, but they did not. And the result opened up a whole world. In meetings and coffee shops, individual members would press upon me their own limits or ideals. But with this passage as my guide, I can easily say that when it comes to sex, I need to search *my* conscience. It's my own sober life and moral choices.

When I first got sober, I worried that sex was also, for me, an addiction. I've looked at that question again and again in years since, especially at times when almost *all* my sexual behavior seemed selfish. Regarding sex, though, addiction hasn't been a useful construct for me. What *is* addiction, after all? I've heard every opinion within A.A. Currently, science says all addiction has related physiological and genetic explanations: differences in chemical levels and neurological responses. I look at my own addictive behaviors and, well, all I can say is that it's complicated.

My relationship to nicotine seems the simplest: keep it out of my body entirely, and it's not an issue. I don't need the program to stay cigarette-free. There don't seem to be any lingering deep-seated psychological issues. I quit, I don't look back; I don't need meetings every day. I don't even gain weight, like so many do. I've tried Nicotine Anonymous meetings, and they were interesting, but in the end, not necessary or even helpful. But after realizing that millions of people would like to stop smoking, it seems the twelve-step model doesn't offer them much assistance in this regard.

Attending Sexual Compulsives Anonymous meetings was more intense for me, but also not helpful. Nicotine and I have a simple, one-dimensional relationship. Sex, by contrast, has had many different *meaning*s for me at different times in the last twenty-four years. My gay identity, emotions, desires, and morals have changed over time. Therapy has been more effective in showing me the reasons for my sexual choices and helping me to make changes in my behavior. "We all have sex problems. We'd hardly be human if we didn't" (*A.A.*, 70).

I've worked at being faithful in a relationship, and hurt someone badly when I didn't succeed. I've had pointless and meaningless sex out of boredom or fear of being alone. I've objectified other men and slept around to avoid facing reality or my own feelings. Though the addiction model hasn't been that useful in understanding my sex life, the actions and principles of A.A., such as honesty and courage, taking inventory and making amends, are effective tools for change in all areas of my life, when I'm willing to use them. "Whatever our ideal turns out to be, we must be willing to grow toward it" (*A.A.*, 70).

With alcohol, the twelve-step model of going to meetings and working the program has kept me sober, though how I've worked my program has changed over time. My New York cocoon was first challenged at about five years sober, when I took a job in a suburb of Philadelphia. Even though I escaped most weekends to my boyfriend back in Chelsea, my cozy routine of meetings and good times with close friends was broken up. This coincided with pulling away from my first sponsor, much as I loved him and had learned from him. Mostly I think it was a natural counter-reaction; after having been so close, I needed to assert my own identity. In Philadelphia, attending but disliking new meetings, I tried to get a local sponsor, someone to help me with the challenges of a new job and a long-distance relationship. I didn't find one; I questioned whether it was my own unwillingness, or just lack of compatibility, but either way, I gave up. Back in

Manhattan just a little more than a year later, I didn't return to my former sponsor/sponsee relationship, either.

In fact, in most of the years since, the large majority of my sober life, I have not called someone "my sponsor," even though many in the program suggest having one for the life of your time in the program. As a newcomer, to have a sponsor was an incredible gift; to be able to call someone every day, talk about myself, knowing he would listen without judgment; to feel someone always had my back. At times, especially when in a new city with new meetings, I've tried to find this resource again; asked someone to be my sponsor, calling regularly, sitting down together to work the steps. Yet these connections never clicked as "sponsorship."

My closest friend, Jim, and I got sober within a few weeks of each other. More than twenty years after each of us last had a drink we still talk several times a week. Sometimes we've agreed that we're each other's sponsors, but that's not really true. We do have an uncanny knack for finding ourselves facing the same issues at the same time, though. To list a few rough patches: jobs, unemployment, financial woes, our families, losing a parent, depression, suicidal thoughts, relationships, fidelity, pornography, other substances, food, weight, body image, illness, loneliness. Our lasting friendship has been a vital part of my staying alcohol-free.

Though I haven't termed anyone my sponsor for most of the last twenty years, I have sponsored many people, working my own twelfth step. Sponsoring two newcomers, Emily and Josh, helped me through the difficult year in Philadelphia. Similar to my own experience, I haven't remained anyone's sponsor throughout the course of his or her sobriety. I have stayed close to Emily, Josh, and other former sponsees for many years, but not remained in that official role. Despite what many believe about the importance of sponsorship, I have found it works best when there are a set of clear issues, like learning to work the steps, for the sponsor and sponsee to address. It has not been necessary in the less dramatic sections of my life.

Different jobs have taken me across the country in the course of my sobriety: after New York, Philadelphia, New York again, Seattle, then New York *again,* then returning to my hometown of Portland for five years, and less than two years ago, moving back up to Seattle. Living in Manhattan and surrounded by friends at groups I loved, going to meetings wasn't an issue; more often I'd wonder if A.A. had just turned into my social life. I enjoyed meetings when I traveled as well, from Paris to Ft. Lauderdale, each place announcing myself as a visitor in a meeting. But when I lived outside of New York, meetings often felt like a chore.

Arriving in a new town, I followed standard suggestions: try different meetings, find a home group, make coffee, help the newcomer, get a sponsor. Nothing much worked. I didn't like the people I met or the way they did things. Each new place, I'd put up with different customs and learn new rituals, introduce myself to strangers, try to make some new friends. Maybe all that activity kept me from drinking or using, but it was infrequently "happy, joyous, and free" (*A.A.*, 133), as the Big Book promises it will be.

Jim and I have talked about this many times, as for both of us our attendance at meetings dwindled in recent years. (Since our first years sober, we've rarely lived in the same city. Jim has relocated from Atlanta to Belgium to Kansas to Poughkeepsie, facing the same difficulties with new meetings.) Just two years ago in Portland, I wondered how much I could still call myself an A.A. member. I felt myself drifting out of contact. First a week or two would go by between meetings. Then maybe a month. On business trips, I'd hit up my old New York home group, but my contact in Portland with other sober people was almost nil. When Jim and I talked, we'd ponder: *Would the day just come when we'd stop going to meetings?* Would we even know when that day came, or would we just look back at some point and realize we couldn't remember the last time we'd been to a meeting?

Our long telephone conversations would get very philosophical. Did we still have a program? Had our love of Alcoholics Anonymous just been a romantic nostalgia for being young and gay in New York, surrounded by our friends? We both had plenty of A.A. acquaintances from early days who went as regularly to meetings as ever. We also both knew guys who'd stopped going to meetings, some long ago. We both could think of people who seemed, from the outside at least, to have learned how to drink in moderation. There were others who were abstinent from drugs or alcohol, but like me without cigarettes, didn't seem to need the daily maintenance of a spiritual program.

One article of faith in A.A., after all, is the disease model of alcoholism. No cure, only a "daily reprieve." Recovering, and not recovered. It's pretty easy to get resentful that you're stuck with a chronic illness. Even in first few months sober, I'd question if this were true. After all, I'd put down the bottle easily enough, and I have been completely alcohol and drug-free since my first meeting. If it was that easy, how could it be a chronic, life-long disease? When my meetings were fun and full of friends, it was one thing; when years later I'd be forcing myself to be honest in a roomful of strangers, it was another. I'd like to be recovered, not feeling guilty if I didn't make meetings, help newcomers, do service, work the steps. What, after all, could I still be getting from meetings, talking year after year about the long ago days when I was a drunk?

Even though I was attending A.A. infrequently, I had no desire to start drinking or using again. But there is no escaping the reality that, in the gay world today, the ravages of drug and alcohol abuse are just as terrible as ever. The soaring use of crystal meth has been especially frightening. On any evening, on any men for men website, there's proof enough of the reality of addiction. Not just in my gay experience but also within my family—I've seen alcohol and drug abuse destroy lives. I can't deny the reality and danger of addiction. And yet, though I was going to meetings less and less, I went, and I still identified with total strangers and what they shared. Meetings reminded me that A.A.'s steps and traditions had been for me "a bridge back to life" and remained a "design for living" (*A.A.*, 81).

I continue to feel that A.A.'s disease model and its twelve steps of recovery were the best tools for combating alcoholism. Even as my active participation shrank to no much more than phone calls, reading, and meditation, I could hold on to A.A.'s Third Tradition, which says the only requirement for membership is a desire to stop drinking, and I remind myself I am a member. My "fellowship of men and women" might have dwindled to Jim and myself, but we were still sharing experience, strength, and hope, and helping each other to recover from alcoholism.

Not quite two years ago, I ended up back in Seattle for yet another job relocation. The professional prospect was great, but I wasn't particularly looking forward to living here again. Ten years earlier, I'd been unhappy and made very few friends, in A.A. or elsewhere. I'd sponsored a couple of guys, and then had completely lost touch with them and felt guilty about that. I had asked someone to be my sponsor, and that had ended with an awkward, painful resentment, and also losing touch. Without much of a program in Portland, though, and a demanding new job, the fellowship of A.A. in Seattle wasn't at the top of my worries.

A few months before the move, Facebook had suggested a couple of "friends" that were Seattle A.A. acquaintances. Even before I was offered the job, I had half-dozen friendships sprouting online. My new office was just down the road from the location of a gay men's meeting, the only one I liked the last time I had lived here. So, I went to it, and five or six guys from the group claimed to remember me (even if I was embarrassed at not remembering them). They reminded me I'd been one of the gang that had helped launch the meeting ten years previously, a detail I had also forgotten.

My new/old friends reached out to invite me to dinner, offered to put me up for the weekend while I apartment hunted, and even found me temporary housing for three months. Suddenly, I had fellowship and a home group again. I was asked to speak at meetings. Soon after my move, I was telling Jim, on the phone, that I was surprised to find myself looking forward to going to meetings again. In fact, with the difficulties of the new job, my Monday group (and dinner before and coffee afterwards) became the highlight of my week.

Just having a weekly home group was more engagement with A.A. than I had had in years. And as it had when I was new, involvement led to more involvement. Over the course of the next year, I went to a nearby Round-Up, which is like a convention of gay sober people. I got reacquainted with even more guys. Men I once thought of as "newcomers" were now celebrating tenth anniversaries. Soon I had a second weekly meeting. I had friends to go to dinner and movies and dancing and opera with. More to the point, I have friends to share with, and my journey through the steps continues. A few months later, I got reacquainted with the man who'd briefly been my sponsor a decade before. Resentments and fears were pushed aside, and now for the first time since my early years, I have a sponsor, whose honesty and help I cherish.

There's more to be grateful for, but the thing is, I never expected any of this. I didn't ask for it and I didn't consciously work for it. But life has brought me here. As it happened, the fantastic new job didn't pan out. The same weekend that my future unemployment became spectacularly and painfully apparent, I was at a retreat with sober friends, surrounded by their love and support. And as the Fellowship usually does, being there helped me a lot.

Life hasn't been a steady upward progression. I may have to move yet again, away from the snug nest Seattle has become. Possibly once more to an unfamiliar city where meetings are different and I don't know anyone in the fellowship.

For me the twelve steps have not been a stairway; they have made a path. In twenty-three sober years I've been well off and broke; deeply in love and single; healthy and bothered by illness. But no matter how circumstances change, time moves on, I get older. Still, "whatever our ideal turns out to be, we must be willing to grow toward it" (*A.A.*, 69). This passage in the Big Book refers to sex; but I take from it how I can approach all of my ideals, my goals or dreams. Instead of giving me a set of rules, Alcoholics Anonymous asks me to look at my choices and judge my own behavior. In the years that I abused alcohol and drugs, I was refusing to admit the truth of my own choices, and hiding from their inevitable consequences. That led to crashing, burning, and landing in A.A.

Without picking up or using, I can, of course, still lie to myself about my behavior and motives. I can ignore or deny the consequences of my choices. And that is why I still use the program in my life.

"We claim spiritual progress, not spiritual perfection. We are not saints. The point is that we are willing to grow along spiritual lines." These lines from chapter five of *Alcoholics Anonymous*, which is called "How It Works." These words are as familiar to me as a church litany. They were read out loud in my first meeting and at most of the meetings I have attended. I probably can recite them in my sleep after hearing them at so many meetings over the years. At my new home group, though, we customarily toss in a few rehearsed comments at certain points in this reading. At that meeting, when I hear, "We are not saints," I also expect to hear a few voices calling, *"What's the point?"* and a collective response, *"The point is that we are willing to grow along spiritual lines."* This is among the various A.A. rituals that vary from room to room, region to region.

And we are supposed to continue to grow. Twenty years after writing the Big Book, Bill W. had some further thoughts about growing up in A.A. "Those adolescent urges that so many of us have for complete approval, utter security, and perfect romance—urges quite appropriate to age seventeen—prove to be an impossible way of life at forty-seven or fifty-seven. Since A.A. began, I've taken huge wallops in all these areas because of my failure to grow up, emotionally and spiritually" (*As Bill Sees It*, 330).

In the years since beginning my own journey in A.A., I have taken my own huge wallops. The point is to continue to grow. "Whatever our ideal turns out to be, we must be willing to grow toward it." The word "must," here, is more than a just a suggestion. "Must" tells me that if I drink or use again, I will stop growing. Flipping that over, it also means that I must try to grow, spiritually, or I will return to alcoholism. Not perfect, not a saint, but wanting to continue to live a life without alcohol, and willing to grow. That is why, nearly twenty-four years later, I remain a member of Alcoholics Anonymous.

If a Bear Gets Sober in the Woods
Wayne H.

My name is Wayne and I'm a recovering alcoholic and drug addict. As I write this, I am less than a month away from celebrating ten years of continuous sobriety. I never thought I'd be able to make a statement like that, but it's close to fruition and it's true. No cocktails, no bong hits, no poppers, no bumps of coke or Special K. No mushrooms or trips on ecstasy or LSD—most of these I gave up more than seventeen years ago the first time I entered the rooms of A.A. I even gave up cigarettes a year and a half into my current recovery, which I consider just as grand an achievement. Though it took three attempts, spanning seventeen years, to get to this landmark, I find that lately my connection to the program has been rather tenuous, even though I know without a doubt I could not have achieved this much clean time without it.

In the rooms of A.A. (M.A., N.A., S.C.A., Al-Anon and so on) I have found strength, courage, and support. Yet, after this much time, the drunkifications I hear at meetings are of little use or interest to me. The so-called glamour of drinking, the parties, the arrests, the abuse of those closest to the user, these are things I have heard over and over, and the more sober I get, the more I notice there seems to be a lot of pride attached to the retelling of these anecdotes. There's some grandiosity in trying to illustrate how dizzying the heights and awesome the depths of one's using history.

These stories were useful to me as a beginner, as they taught me that we all use in similarly, and for a very few common reasons. However, as I gained clarity and focus, it became far more important for me to hear how sober people with clean time stuck to their guns. I wanted to know how they managed life through its many ups and downs, over an extended period of time. And how they did it staying clean and sober. In the meetings I attend, these stories seem few and far between! Although hearing gratitude and the practice of the first three steps echoed in newcomer qualifications has a lot of value, at this point in my sobriety I find it hard to listen to this yet again. It doesn't make me feel connected.

I consider my own drinking and using story to be hopelessly mundane; I believe I am more useful and of service when I recount the ways in which I have been able to put what I have learned in twelve-step programs to practical use, living as an openly gay man in New York City. My using history and my adult sexuality are closely tied. I grew up in New York, but I first started getting stoned on grass in college, in the earliest weeks of my freshman year of college in faraway Ohio. I really felt like a fish out of water, away from home for the first time.

Soon, I connected with a couple of the other boys on the floor of my dorm, getting drunk on cheap wine on the very first weekend, and began smoking pot somewhere in the first month. I was starting to ache with the knowledge that I was gay and began to have feelings for one of my best male friends. But I needed the camaraderie that was developing amongst all of the guys, and I didn't want to do anything to threaten that. For me, at this pivotal time in my life, being liked was all-important. I wasn't even completely sure about how gay sex worked (I hadn't even seen gay porn yet) and in high school I actively and doggedly put the whole notion of homosexuality off. I really thought of it as an affliction that affected a very small number of people; a notion I wouldn't shake until I attended my first Gay Pride parade.

Getting high plunged feelings down a mental toilet, allowing me to put off dealing with ideas that were still unsettling. I'd known at least since puberty that I *might* prefer boys to girls, but I just did not want to really force myself to ponder this question or resolve it at the time. In high school, I had struggled for social acceptance and wanted to be one of the popular kids; the feeling became even more pressing at college, when I was so far removed from everything I'd ever known before. I made a very conscious decision to put off the matter of my sexuality until I got to college, as I knew that I was getting out of my parents' house and far away to the Midwest, and I'd be making a great separation with my life then. I'd have the chance to re-invent myself there.

When it finally happened, when I made a romantic and physical connection with another boy at the age of nineteen, I remember feeling giddy and just a bit reborn. I felt part of a special secret club. I have strong sense memory of coming back from my first lover's off-campus apartment at dawn in early spring, smelling like him, knowing I had crossed an amazing threshold into an exciting new world of which my friends back at the dorm knew nothing. For the remainder of my years in college I enjoyed a healthy sex life and a succession of boyfriends. I was very fortunate to be at an extremely liberal and gay friendly college that worked to educate us about HIV and AIDS, had a very visible Gay/Lesbian/Bi Alliance and an ACT UP! chapter, and which attracted lots of gay boys and girls! I used throughout college, jumping from pot to LSD and mushrooms, but my drug of choice for the most part was pot. Drinking was not a love of mine, as I tended to vomit and I just didn't enjoy the unpredictability of what I might say or do when drunk.

Transitioning from a sheltered idyllic life on campus to adult life back in New York City was very difficult. Financial circumstances found me living back with my family in the Bronx housing project apartment I grew up in. I was separated from all the friends I'd made, and did not have the wherewithal to try and find my way in the city's vast gay community. I smoked a lot of pot and drank occasionally to deal with the depression and isolation. My mom was lenient about the pot, at least at first. I didn't like the nagging comments she made when she noticed it was a very regular, daily habit. Eventually I would get out of the Bronx and move to Brooklyn, where I shared an apartment with a sober gay man. I had very little understanding of what that meant. By then I was an everyday smoker and had picked up cigarettes as well.

My using accelerated when one of my college friends moved into the neighborhood. He introduced me to cocaine and to the club life. By following closely behind him, I regularly gained entrance to clubs and got on the all-important guest lists. Once again, I felt a part of something special. It was pretty unreal, being able to smoke grass and snort coke completely in the open in the club environment at that particular moment in New York City nightlife. Using and getting high, like coming out of the closet before it, seemed the rarified province of the truly fabulous and important on the face of the earth!

This feeling would be replicated when I entered A.A., which truly is an exclusive club for people who want to be well. The tension between feeling *apart from* and feeling *a part of* has been a part of my life for as long as I can remember, intensified with the successive experiences of coming out and becoming sexually active as a gay man, learning to use my various qualifying substances, and coming into A.A. to get sober three times.

Cocaine hooked me instantly, and I was aware that I was an addict from my first use, even though I confined my use to weekends.

Where pot soothed my rage, coke flattened many remaining negative feelings and eliminated all physical aches and pains as a special added bonus. Coke made me feel invincible. It definitely seemed to me that I had arrived as a gay man, and gay life revolved around these dancing and drug rituals. Sex, however, rarely came into play, as I was really only focused on getting my drugs and getting high. My masturbatory life was actually very exciting and even with the pot, coke, and poppers it was very reliable. Where sex was concerned, dealing with other people was far too difficult to bother with. I was ignorant (fortunately?) of all the sex going on around me, I had little knowledge of the bathhouses and backrooms.

After a year of life on the club scene, it was time to surrender to sobriety. There were no arrests or injuries, no hospitals or institutions; just the pain of knowing I was enslaved to my substances and that I wasn't dealing with life. I had been laid off from my first post-college corporate position and was floating aimlessly, spiritually and physically, couch-surfing and really only focused on the weekend, which is when I used coke and ecstasy. I was twelve-stepped, which is program lingo that means I was led into the rooms, by the boyfriend of a guy who I'd done drugs and danced with. He was a high school teacher who was recovering from being a junkie (!) and I had left some of my stuff at his apartment. He could see what condition when I arrived after being up all night and he gently but clearly recommended A.A. At the very same time, an old high school girlfriend who had been a pot smoking buddy had started going to M.A. meetings and was also suggesting that I check that out.

I recall very little about my very first meeting other

than the when and where, and being made to feel at home. It was a roomful of gay men, many of them very attractive, and they welcomed me with open arms. Some were doing the kissy-huggy thing for hellos and goodbyes. I had been celibate for quite some time, as my need to get high had surpassed my need to meet guys. At one meeting I went to during my first week, a handsome man gave me a hug, and I thought it meant I had a boyfriend. During the same meeting I was cruised and picked up by a guy who I thought was going to teach me "the Program." He actually pretended to call the friend who brought me to the meeting and got his approval for the hook up! He then kicked his boyfriend out of their studio and tried to fuck me without a condom.

I would learn shortly thereafter that this was an A.A. no-no, and that the people in the program, and the Program of A.A., were two different things. Thus was born my first sober resentment.

I stayed sober for twenty months, working a minimal program, and relapsed when I found a (somewhat sober) boyfriend and a job. I had the cash and prizes I was lacking when I'd arrived in the rooms: job, apartment, boyfriend. Now long-repressed feelings were starting to surface, fellowship was becoming work, and I just had no time for any of it. I nestled into a pretty co-dependent relationship and that took all my time and effort.

I briefly got sober again about three years into this relationship, but even though it was largely stagnant and negative by this time, I was still too wrapped up in it, and in him, to really pay any heed to what I was seeing and hearing at meetings. No commitments were made, no new friends gained. I pieced together eleven very forgettable months of not using, and started smoking pot again after he moved out.

I came back to A.A. after a year and a half, after

living through the events of 9/11 showed me very clearly how small my world had become since deciding to be a stoner again. In effect, my coming in and out of sobriety always had to do with relationships, and with the notion of being a part of something larger than myself, versus the utter isolation of using. Sometimes being gay seemed like a magical doorway into secret exciting worlds; but now it set me apart from the rest of the world, as in the case of my straight friends who were starting to marry, move to the 'burbs and procreate. I was glued to my couch and TV, sexless and in exile from gay New York.

Another reason I decided to get sober again was a loss of physical coordination, which I attributed to my incessant pot-smoking. I would regularly have accidents like when I injured my knee walking into the jutting spout of a fire hydrant. Another and much stronger impetus to get sober was a pending case in housing court. Squirrels had taken up residence in the space between my ceiling and the roof, and one had died inside a wall, creating an unforgettable odor that made me sick—I was compelled to take steps to address the situation. Even in my pot-addled condition, I had learned from A.A. how to ask for and accept help, and to always take the next right step.

My date in court was during the first week of my new sobriety. I had also decided (VERY unwisely) to restart myself on my anti-depressant that week without the advice of a physician. I was very afraid of court, and really believed at the time that all judges were like Judge Judy. I was terrified of losing. I had spent a long time couch-surfing and wanting my own apartment during the years I was a club kid, and had suffered through some hideous roommate situations before finally getting this place with an ex-boyfriend. After we broke up, wresting the lease from my ex was a drama.

I felt it was of the utmost importance to fight for my

space, and the possibility of losing, of being humiliated or humbled in front of the landlord's people was torturous. I remember waking up that morning and wishing that I would be hit by a bus or fall into a hole because I was so wracked by fear! But, I did show up, and I even called my Mommy to come with me as backup. Thankfully, the judge was revolted by my landlord's unwillingness to properly address the situation, and she ordered him to remedy the problem immediately, without any trial. I felt very relieved and vindicated, as the landlord's attorney was attempting to portray me as a "prima donna" for not wanting to live with vermin! Even in relapse there were some things I took from my first attempt at sobriety that stayed with me, simple things like showing up for myself, and taking the next right action made a difference. I can't ever forget how afraid I was that day, I was choking on fear, but I knew to show up, have a little faith in the actions I took, and turn over the results.

Certainly that powerful fear I felt would have been greatly reduced if I had been sober. But I was not, and later that week, I found myself on the roof of my building, in a screaming fight with an elderly woman from the adjacent tenement, yelling obscenities at her and vowing to have her put into an asylum or an old age home. I discovered that she was putting out treats and food on her fire escape for the pigeons and squirrels, the latter making their way into the infrastructure of her building and from hers into mine. The police arrived and wanted to know what prompted me to call an old woman a cunt. This kind of scene is *not* a part of my life in sobriety!

I started my current round of sobriety by making a very wise decision to focus my energy on making friends and not love connections. This really worked for me and was key to my success that first year and beyond. Having sober "girlfriends" to talk to and hang with really made a difference in the quality of my sobriety, as opposed to my first effort in the rooms. I had been sexless for a very long time prior to coming back, so it was hard to stuff down my lust. Getting involved in sticky relationship drama was key to my failure the first time around, so I was determined to learn from that mistake. I tried hard to learn how to relate to other gay men, even very attractive ones, on a level that was not charged with sex.

In meetings, I listened much harder than I'd ever done before, and actually worked to use what I was learning in real life. I utilized a series of increasingly more wisely chosen sponsors and read into the literature far more than I'd ever done on the last go-round.

I have memories of a lot of post-meeting meals with a group for fellowship. There were numerous opportunities to apply many of the principles learned in the Big Book, and gleaned from shares and qualifications in meetings. But also there were examples of dysfunction. I recall one of my friends hurling an extremely biting comment at another, and though I burned with embarrassment for both, I didn't comment or get involved because it was not about me. On other occasions I became very stressed when there were over a dozen of us at dinner after the meeting, trying to sort out who would sit near whom and at which table, as there were various persons at odds with various others. On at least two occasions, when I found the assortment of personalities at my table excruciatingly unacceptable, I excused myself to have a cigarette and never returned! I had trouble finding a sponsor, and tried several on for size. The first two didn't work out, and I and let them go, in a sober way, and I was surprised to find that I had to deflect *their* reactions, which were emotional and accusatory.

I was proud to get through these situations without firing back or getting angry. I knew that it was my job, especially as a beginner, to focus on myself. One sponsor was leaning back on me in what I felt was a very inappropriate way; another was a little too unavailable (in the days just prior to cell phones becoming commonplace). When it got to be too much, I simply got up and walked out on fellowship scenes where I just couldn't conquer my discomfort.

I learned to put down or walk away from friendships that weren't working, where I wasn't getting what I asked for or needed. There were no mean e-mails or screaming phone calls anymore, these decisions were always discussed with my sponsor and other sober pals at the time, and dealt with maturely.

I was a regular at meetings, I took service positions, and even got my first sponsee whom I adored. Again, I marveled at how I could feel love and affection for another gay man and not have it commingled with sexual desire. Though I am sure I wasn't the best sponsor in the world, I was available to him, and it felt good to pass on what I had learned.

I would eventually stress to my sponsee that it was his privilege, and *responsibility*, to choose the people he really wanted around him. He was very sensitive to people with "reduced boundaries," and I told him that though we were all sick and suffering, he should move towards people who made him feel safe and whose recovery seemed attractive. It is my experience that A.A. works better when you stick with the "winners." Winners are members who are working the program in a way that seems to serve their growth, serenity, and happiness. Only when I learned these things for myself could I successfully attempt to pass them on to a newcomer.

Around the year-and-a-half mark, I encountered a challenge that nearly broke my sobriety, a romantic obsession. The details of his story are unimportant, except that he was returning from a slip, was very damaged, and for reasons that hark back to my having addiction in the intimate family setting, I was seized with the need to save him. There was physical attraction and want of course, but I think the need to fix and help him was more engrossing, especially after he relapsed. I was sure that I loved him and that he loved me back, even though it was largely unsaid and unexpressed. I was one of the only people he reached out to during his relapse, and I watched heartbroken as his life started to disintegrate. I was crushed when his job finally dismissed him, and held back tears as he related the incident without emotion.

I couldn't tell that he was high, even though we would stay up all night. I was unfamiliar with crystal meth and didn't understand what it was doing to him. I knew that his world was very small, but I was part of it. When he came back from the slip, my obsession spun out of control. He was paranoid, disoriented and hard to deal with. Worse, he showed sexual interest in one of my friends and my new sponsee. I knew I had to seek help, as the feelings I was having around this relationship were just unbearable.

The lengths I went to seek help to this day are a landmark of my sobriety. I shared openly and honestly in meetings, and with friends and sponsor about what was going on. I even remember speaking to a friend's sponsor. I started going to an Al-Anon Double Winners meeting, and to an S.C.A. meeting that focused on romantic obsession (the luxury of meetings such as these is one of the many advantages of being sober in a city like New York). I prayed to be relieved of the obsession, which gripped my first thoughts in the morning and my last thoughts at night. My willingness to seek and ask for help, and my desire to be healthy, eventually led me to cut this man from my life altogether, which did break the obsession. When I was able to put some distance between us, I was better able to figure out why I was focusing on him.

I embrace the program slogan, "If it's hysterical, it's historical," and I was able to look at my family's addiction to see what this relationship had represented for me. I was able to see that he manipulated me, and my reactions to him, to keep me taking care of him. I remember what it felt like to miss a call from him... I literally put him before anyone and anything else. In the end, because I was willing to use the tools I was handed: meetings, fellowship, sponsorship, service, and literature, I was able to effectively seek help and healing. I had developed a nice relationship with a Higher Power as well, and relied on that channel too.

Around this time, I was presented with an opportunity to be on a popular TV makeover show. This came through the program, as one of my sober friends was working on the show and was getting word out that a gay guy was needed for a makeover. Initially, sloth and apathy set in. I just didn't feel like doing the interview. I never imagined I could be chosen for such a thing.

I always had a soft spot for the little A.A. slogans and anagrams. I feel they are shortcuts to bigger ideas. At the time of the audition, I was enamored of two anagrams: H.O.W. and H.A.G., which stood for Honesty/Openness/ Willingness and Humility/Acceptance/Gratitude. I had mentioned them in qualifications and now applied them to the situation. I did the interview and had great chemistry with the producer. She called me the next day to make arrangements to see my apartment, as it was going to be a central focus of the makeover. And when they told me I was chosen, over so many others, I was thrilled beyond belief.

A roadblock emerged to my doing the show, as the landlord's permission had to be obtained, and we were not on great terms, owing to our now two trips to housing court. I wrote a heartfelt letter to him, promising to be the model tenant if he would only give the green light to this project. He did relent, but not because of my exercise in humility: he took a cash payoff from the producers.

I told the show from the get-go that I did not drink, but I did not specify that I was in recovery. The show remade slovenly or goofy straight men over according to gay male sensibility, and I was to be its first gay makeover, in an episode for Gay Pride month. Drinking is very ingrained into gay culture; indeed, the show had alcohol companies as sponsors. I was very concerned with maintaining my anonymity as per the traditions; in the end I was taught how to make a cocktail and appeared to drink one as well, though it was virgin.

Having a camera in my face all day for three days made getting to meetings a challenge. Also, I was forbidden contact with my friends during the makeover process, so I had to go to meetings where I wouldn't know anyone. In the end, the show was fun to tape, and I was very unconscious of the camera and felt pretty comfortable. I had decided at the outset to do whatever was asked of me, and indeed, some of the dialogue revolved around me being willing to take chances. I snuck in program talk about openness and willingness! Program friends filled the venue where the climactic segment was shot. I had actually received literal cash and prizes and was elated. I felt very much indebted to sobriety for the experience.

There were a lot of very important upshots from the makeover experience. As a result of my "fifteen minutes," I began going out much more, enjoying the recognition I received after the show aired. I now had two sponsees, one of whom was in the show, and I felt I was being a good example of what gifts sobriety could bring. This was a very golden time for me, as I was working the program perhaps to the fullest I'd ever done before or since; and I had a connection to a Higher Power that was very consistent and new to me. I felt very rewarded by the special opportunity I'd been given, and I also received material gifts as well. In doing the reality show, I had opened myself to the unknown, and I remember promising myself I'd do anything the producers wanted me to – if it meant having my back waxed or skydiving, I'd do it. The camera exposed and objectified me in a way I'd never experienced before.

After the show I started going out dancing and to bars, and this meant looking at guys and considering sex again. I was adamant about not returning to the places I went when I was a club kid. With certain friends egging me on and accompanying me, I finally felt emboldened to step into the world of gay casual sex.

I had lost a lot of weight between the end of my relationship and doing the TV show and I felt good enough about my looks and body to get out and have a little fun. Eventually, I became addicted to the reality that sex could be had in this city anytime, anywhere. My behaviors became darker and I took unnecessary chances. This period was thankfully short-lived. I'm grateful for not having been harmed or harmed myself, and frankly it was very freeing and important for me to rediscover myself as a sexual being. The relationship that I lost my sobriety over, which then prompted me in and out of the program twice more, had been largely sexless and really damaged my self-esteem and ramped up my body image issues. I felt like I took on some of his issues and hang-ups too. Once again, one of my favorite program anagrams pertained to something I had been through: RELATIONSHIP = Real Exciting Love Affair Turns Into Outrageous Nightmare; Sobriety Hangs in Peril!

Eventually the cruising and back rooms became mundane, and the acting out ebbed. I was definitely open about what I was going through in meetings, sharing in a general way about how I'd found a new using experience, and how it was making me feel. In hindsight, I feel this was a necessary phase for me to go through, as the hang-ups and baggage from my program and relapse history needed working through. I also received a lot of positive reinforcement about my appearance, even as I gained back a lot of my weight and grew into a "bear." I learned that there was more room inside the gay community for men past thirty (and then forty!), and in different shapes and sizes, than I had imagined.

The aftermath of doing the show also brought on a massive feeling of disillusionment, which led in turn to a break in the relationship I'd established with my Higher Power. I had actually cherished the notion that I'd be "discovered" on the show, and with my sparkling wit and personality end up having my own morning talk show on Logo. Instead, the makeover show editors were very careful to make me as *schleppy* as possible, to enhance the impact of the makeover. Anytime I got too cute or witty, those moments were cut. In fact, one of the producers told me very clearly before we started that the makeover guys were the stars of the show, not I.

As the show's airing became more and more a memory, I realized that I had not achieved stardom, nor had I had any marriage proposals. I had engaged in a lot of sex, but rarely any dates and certainly no one to fall in love with. I remember talking to my sponsor at the time about the great distance I had come to feel between me and my Higher Power. We traced it back to the show. I came to see that I had some very grand hopes that were unfulfilled and I felt a profound sense of disappointment. This is something that has only intensified in the intervening years.

By this time in my sobriety I had a very good understanding of the steps and traditions, and in response to this overpowering feeling of disenchantment, I tried hard to put them to work in my daily life. I had also gotten some really good stuff out of the Al-Anon meetings I went to, as I still struggled to cope with relationships of all types.

Small nuggets implant themselves easiest in my brain. This is why I like slogans – they allow me to learn that "not everything was about me," and "to keep it simple." I learned to "say what I mean and mean what I say." I learned to "get right-sized," which for me was not about grandiosity but about finding my voice. I began to ask for what I needed in relationships and if I couldn't get it, I walked away without rancor.

I learned to "keep my side of the street as clean as possible," and I have had opportunity to put this to healthy use. A co-worker, with whom I'd been having tension, finally exploded one day when I refused to let her bully me. I stood quietly while she ranted to our boss, and when she let loose the F-word, "Faggot!" I declared that my workday was done and simply walked away. Because I was sober and had learned not to engage, I did not respond to her like I did to the elderly woman on my roof, and her rage led her to self-destruct. When I left work, I made a few phone calls, including one to my sponsor, and when I returned the next day she was fired. If I had not been sober and practicing the steps, the rage I worked so hard to tamp down with pot, cigarettes, and coke would most surely have been triggered by her slur, and I would have fired back a few of my own, made the scene far worse, and perhaps have been penalized myself. The very simplest lessons I learned in A.A., amassed from shares and meetings, were the ones that served me best.

After the sixth or seventh year of sobriety, friends

started drifting away. They were relapsing, moving, shifting programs, or dying. I found myself haunted by their ghosts in meetings. I saw the empty spaces where they used to sit. This is when qualifications became difficult to listen to, the drinking stories were repetitive, and many of the same people were choosing each other to speak ad nauseum.

I found myself very strongly resenting people who had accumulated some decent sober time and still spent the bulk of their qualification on their using stories. As I said before, I wanted to hear how people *lived* in sobriety. Little things in meetings became distracting and irritating, a newcomer breathing on me, people eating and texting. One meeting actually took a "group conscience" at the beginning of every meeting to decide whether or not to have air conditioning in the summer or an open door. Invariably, young, thin, hairless queens would vote to shut off the a/c, which always left me sweating and dripping, and resentful as hell.

Because my meetings had thinned and I wasn't working much of a program, I got sloppy with some of the core programmatic lessons for my everyday life. I really had mastered restraint of pen and tongue, and I had thought I learned that just because I had something to say didn't mean that it needed to be heard. But during this time, in self-righteous rage, I posted a hard jab at a coworker on Facebook, heedless of the fact that several of my coworkers would see it. Though the slight was against an unnamed and ungendered individual, my coworkers correctly deduced the identity of the target of my disdain and alerted Management. I was mortified, and I was disciplined. The workplace environment would now always have a touch of that shame for me.

I handled the situation the best I could, went to a meeting, asked for help, and spoke my mind to my superiors when I was given the opportunity. The idea that I was disciplined for a Facebook posting still burns; but the simple fact that I forgot to restrain my pen/tongue is undeniable. The fear I felt while waiting for my "punishment" reminded me of the fear I felt on my way to court that morning during my first sober week. In many ways that experience was like a slip to me!

Though my immersion in A.A. has waned over the last few years, I value my sobriety enormously. I believe I have learned to be teachable. I try my best to always do the next right thing and let go of the results. I feel that I have become a more compassionate person, having come to realize that we are all sick and suffering to varying extents. I try my best to ask for help and ask for what I need, though this is something I struggle with. I try to remember that relationships are what you bring to them and not what you get from them. I try not to lead with my mouth. When someone tells me they are unavailable, either explicitly or through their actions, I listen. One sponsor taught me, "You train people how to treat you." When it comes to phone or electronic messages, no answer *is* an answer.

I have tried to take all this to heart. I once again teetered on the edge of romantic obsession, but recalling how I suffered that long year, and how hard I had to work to get a grip on those feelings, I pulled back from the person. It's like relapsing with many other diseases. Once one has learned how and when to get medicine, the illness isn't as severe or long lasting as the time before. I recalled the slogan that "Man's rejection is God's protection."

One of my most difficult dilemmas today is fitting the concept of a Higher Power into my life, something that is completely baffling me. For a brief period early in my sobriety, I had really embraced the notion of a benevolent all-seeing entity watching over me. I prayed on a daily basis, as I did when I was a child, not for protection from a list of movie monsters, nor for material things, but for strength and courage, and for the ability to be of service to myself and others. I fondly recall giving a very heartfelt second step qualification and talking about how I came to believe. But, at some point after taping the TV show, my faith wavered. The post-fifteen-minutes-of-fame letdown was so overwhelming; and more disappointments cropped up and multiplied.

When I segued from casual sex and tried dating, the disappointments reached epic proportions. Higher Power was now the entity mercilessly seeing to it that not only did I not have someone to love (by way of sending me on an infinite number of horrendous first dates) but on a daily basis punished me with catastrophes in all shapes and sizes, from missed buses to lost/broken/dropped objects, a non-stop parade of bumps, cuts, bruises, and minor illness; and financial woes I have yet to resolve. A sage queen we dubbed "The Empress" once said that if you are not feeling loved and protected by your Higher Power, you fire the bitch and start over! The problem for me has been modifying my idea of what HP should be.

Even as I struggle with this question, I find I have much to be grateful for. I do have sober friends in my life. I make my bed every day and strive to be kind to myself. I know I am not the best sober example, no shining beacon. I am still very much a person that must flee the fire, rather than move freely towards the light! The fact remains that I am clean and sober, after many, many one-days-at-a-time. That is something I try not to take for granted. I know that I am in the minority. I cannot ever forget this. One of my first friends in sobriety has been in a dark crystal meth relapse for quite some time, and it is so difficult to accept powerlessness over his illness. That could be me.

I know this because I find myself hungry for more

support than I can find in meetings alone. Above and beyond all else, there is one way I stay focused on my own sobriety. I try earnestly to be a power of example to anyone watching, never preaching, generally keeping my anonymity, but always ready to share the benefit of my experiences.

I am still struggling with my relationship with a Higher Power; I still find meetings tedious; and at present am lacking sponsor and sponsees. Still, I have sober people in my life and plenty of sober references. I like to think I've learned from my most hideous mistakes and I definitely feel that being clean and sober is the foundation to anything else I might aspire to or achieve. Ten years is a long time to any newcomer trying to squeak out that first twenty-four; but from this view, it's gone by rather quickly. The memory of what it "used to be like," coupled with hearing my once-clean best friend desperately try to make a go of living with addiction, in a futile attempt to make it work. These remind me of the pain that I know awaits if I choose to slide backwards instead of moving forward.

A Sober Leatherman
Edge

If you had asked me five years ago, "What are you?" my answer would have been definitive: I'm a leatherman. In saying that, I would not have meant that I was a gay man who had sex in leather, though that's certainly a part of it. Rather, I would be positioning myself within a rich culture and community, one with its own set of values, aesthetics, traditions, and expectations. Being a leatherman wasn't only reflected in what I did in the bedroom (well, playroom); it was also reflected in how I dressed each day, how I carried myself, and how I treated others. Being a leatherman was a core part of my identity, a foundation for how I saw myself as I moved through the world.

Ask me the same question today and my answer is very different: I'm an alcoholic. Actually, alcohol was only one of my problems, but alcoholism aptly names my disease. In saying I'm an alcoholic I don't simply mean that I am someone with a drinking problem. As with being a leatherman, it means membership in a community and an entirely new way of seeing myself in relation to the world around me. For me, the movement from "leatherman" to "alcoholic" was the "entire psychic change" discussed in "The Doctor's Opinion" of the Big Book. I had to completely reorganize my identity, exchanging one cornerstone (one which I had spent years laying and building upon) for a new foundation and understanding of who I am. This is the story of how I learned to integrate those two parts of myself. This is the story of how I became a sober leatherman.

I was very fortunate when I entered the twelve-step rooms. My city has a gay recovery clubhouse (a luxury I know not everyone has), so that was where I headed when I first admitted to myself that I needed help. When I entered the rooms and looked around, I never saw myself. Initially, then, I felt very "apart from" rather than "a part of." There was a kind of subcultural gulf between me and those others. Yes, we were all gay, but we were different *kinds* of gay: we didn't go to the same bars, didn't hang with the same people, never attended the same parties. They were clean-shaven, I was bearded. They wore sandals, I wore boots. In those first few meetings, every fiber of my being told me to *run*—not because I looked so different from everyone else but because fear was my default mode of life. I knew this about myself, so I didn't run. But I also didn't take the program very seriously. Instead, like any pigheaded drunk, I white knuckled it for six months with no sponsor, no steps, no prayer, no Higher Power, and only about one meeting a week. In those days, leather was something like armor for me: it kept me safe from those others in the room because I just wasn't ready to admit we were all the same.

Then I relapsed (of course). And I'll tell you this—it was *good*. Short, sweet, fun, and consequence free. I remember the next day, remember distinctly telling myself, "Nobody has to know, ever." But then I had an honest moment—my first real moment of clarity. I could see the road and where it led. Yes, I got away with it this time, but suddenly I knew I would do it again, and again, and again, and then some day I'd just be dead. Finally

105

seeing the road, I decided it was time to take a different path.

That path was right back into the rooms. I relapsed on a Friday night. On Tuesday I headed back to the clubhouse and ran into someone I knew from the meetings. He asked me how I was; I told him I had relapsed. He asked if I talked to my sponsor, I told him I didn't have one. He said I should get one, and I said five words that changed my life: *Will you be my sponsor?* He had this look on his face, like he had really stepped in it, but he agreed. Somewhere in that process, I started to surrender. It wasn't easy. Let's face it —leather and control are a natural match and one I had pretty much mastered. Calling someone every day, taking suggestions. These were not easy things for me. But I did them. And they saved my life.

For once I did a real "ninety-in-ninety," one twelve-step meeting a day for three months. I still showed up in my big Wesco boots with a hanky in my pocket. Somewhere after my first thirty days or so, I stopped *looking* for people like me and started *listening* for people like me. Once I did, I realized that no matter how different we seemed to be, I was like them, they were like me, and if I did what they did, I could stay sober. But it was more than that. I might have looked different but people went out of their way to make sure I didn't *feel* different. I remember one old timer asking me about my hanky color and what it meant; I remember someone commenting on my leather wristband and the fact I was a Top; I remember showing up to speak at a meeting in a local rehab facility, in eighteen-inch boots, and having the chair compliment me on them. I'll be honest, that chair kept me coming back because he accepted me, asked how I was doing, gave me a smile when he saw me at meetings, and let me know I was OK just where I was. I never felt excluded and never felt like a freak. So whaddya know, it turns out that "let us love you until you can love yourself" stuff isn't bullshit after all. When I stopped judging everyone else I realized no one was judging me. My recovery had truly begun.

Still, I had this leather thing. What was I to do with *that?* In the meetings I attend, discussing sex at all is a bit taboo, somehow perceived as diverting the group from its primary purpose. I always find that ironic, considering how openly the Big Book discusses sex. Just check page sixty-nine: "We remembered always that our sex powers were God-given." As I point out to my sponsees, when doing a fourth step, a fearless and moral personal inventory, you don't have a separate sheet for lying or stealing but you do have one for sexual harms. The founders of A.A., I think, realized that sex has enormous potential—to hurt or to heal, to create or destroy, to grow, or devolve. But somehow that understanding never made it to the meetings I attended. That's just fine, really. I had enough work to do just staying sober. The leather thing hung above me but my recovery was before me, and so that's where I placed my energy and attention.

A crucial step in this process was when I decided to put everything in my life on the table: my job, my relationship, my leather, where I lived, where I went, who my friends were. I put it all there and I asked my Higher Power to take away those things that threatened my sobriety. That, for me, was my true moment of surrender and as I devoted myself to that offering I came to live my first three steps. As part of that process, I kept my job; changed my relationship; let go of certain people, places, and things; and put leather up on the shelf. For the first six months of my sobriety, I didn't wear it, didn't look for it, didn't have sex in it (didn't have much sex at all, really), and certainly didn't go to the local leather bar. Instead, I called my sponsor, prayed every morning and every night, and went to a meeting every day. Leather was once a part of my daily life—I wore boots every day, even in the middle of a Florida summer—but that space increasingly was supplanted with the job of saving my life.

My psychic change started.

As I grew in the program it continued. Where once I would haltingly, shamefully say I was an alcoholic, I came to announce it with something akin to pride. I grew a new community of friends in the rooms. I put my program first and let everything fall into place behind it. My alcoholism was always central. To this day, when I go to meetings I don't say my name and then say I'm an alcoholic; for me it's the other way around: "I'm an alcoholic and my name is…."

Where once my identity and life were organized around being a leatherman, they came to be organized around being an alcoholic in recovery. When I ate dinner was determined by what meeting I was going to go to. When I woke up the first thing I did was make my bed, because that was what my sponsor suggested I do. When I traveled I looked up what meetings I could make. I called three people every day, not looking to hook up but to connect to others in recovery. The core of my identity changed and my life along with it. I'm glad I had the courage to put leather on the table and also glad that I put it there for as long as I did. It wasn't just that I needed the time and energy to learn how to be a recovering alcoholic. It's also that I needed to start learning who I really was—the me behind the leather. I needed to learn how to stop hating myself, stop killing myself, and—if not start loving—at least start liking myself. Putting leather aside let me do all that. Without the armor, I let people in. I let myself out.

I don't think it was until one of my first "God moments" that I started exploring leather again. I don't remember all the details or the context but I do remember a very clear message coming into my mind some time in my first year of recovery, somewhere around the six month mark: *Do not be afraid of what you are.* To this day, I continue to tease out all the meanings of those words: do not be afraid of being an alcoholic, do not be afraid of being gay, do not be afraid of being a lover, do not be afraid of being a brother and a son, do not be afraid of, well, life. But the meaning that was clearest to me at the time was that I didn't have to be afraid of being a leatherman. It was a message from my Higher Power. It was permission to return to that part of me.

So I dipped my toe back into the waters. I unpacked and conditioned my leathers. I shined up my boots. Having organized my identity around being an alcoholic in recovery, it was time to figure out where and how being a leatherman fit into this vision of the new me. It's probably something I should have discussed with my sponsor but while I was a great sponsee in terms of calling every day (at 8:00 p.m., promptly) and completing all assignments (first 164 pages of the Big Book? Finished them! What's next?), I was not so great with the trusting and sharing thing. I didn't even discuss it much with my best friend in recovery. As close as we were, we were also as different as night and day (in fact, one of the things I love about recovery is that almost none of my friends are like me). I talked about it with my partner, who's kinky like me, but a "normie," free from the disease of alcoholism. That's about it; otherwise, I made the decision to re-enter the leather world on my own. Being a sponsor now, it's the kind of thing I hope my sponsees would discuss with me, as I would hope they would feel safe discussing with me any decision or issue that could impact their sobriety. It's also the kind of thing I completely understand and forgive them for when they don't. Having made my own mistakes, I have the courage to let my sponsees make theirs. I try to be there for them at the end of it, for good or bad.

In some ways I was lucky. The more my disease had progressed, the more I had retreated from the leather community and the more I self-isolated. By the time I was hitting my bottom, I was already, really, out of the "scene." The luck in that was the fact that my leather life had never been deeply intertwined with the people, places, and things that drove me to the rooms. The luck was that I could wade back into the waters without encountering triggers. I reconnected with friends first. After all, through the steps I was finally figuring out what it meant to be a friend in the first place.

Sex came next. Tentative, scary, sporadic. I tried out scenes. Some felt great and some felt awful. Sometimes I would feel right and good about what had happened, as though the sex had honored all involved, but other times I would feel awful, knowing that I had had sex for the wrong reasons (to escape, to validate, to get something). Without substances, I found fear—a *lot* of it. I felt awkward in scenes where once I felt perfectly in command. At the same time, it suddenly dawned on me that there was another person there in those scenes, someone with their own needs, desires, fantasies, and expectations. Self-seeking started to slip away.

Back then I didn't have all the tools of the steps, but I did have prayer. I used it constantly. I can remember, in fact, the first time it all "clicked" for me. The local bondage club was having a party. This time, I *did* talk to my sponsor about it. And then I prayed. And then I prayed some more. I asked my Higher Power to be with me, to guide me, to protect me. I surrendered and asked only for the will of my Higher Power for that evening. The party itself was a bit of a bust—lots of sex in dark corners but very little actual bondage. I chatted with a few guys and kept my prayer tools at the ready. One guy I chatted with seemed OK, but the more we chatted I realized he was really more than OK. I told him about being in recovery (I *always* talk about that before sex) and he was cool with it. We talked some more and then headed back to his place to play most of the night. I remember the joy in the morning. I remember the joy of knowing it could happen—kink and spirit, leather and sober. I remembered the *hope* of it. It is hope that always has, and always will, sustain me.

Still, the journey has not always been easy. This may sound perverse to some, but I often invite my Higher Power into scenes with me. I ask for His guidance. It keeps me present. As I grew in recovery I realized that too often sex, play, kink, love, and intimacy were all very different things for me. And yet I still struggle with being present in sex, particularly in the context of my relationship. It's something I am learning how to do with him slowly, and in the meantime I've always been and always will be "Sir" to my "cub." What's helped is that we talk about it. I tell him how scared I am in sex, how hard it is to be present, how awkward I really am in my body behind all the leather. He listens and supports. I can only do that because today I know how to be honest. That came from the steps. In fact, all the progress I've made around sex and intimacy has come from working the steps. I can be honest about what I want and what I don't want, I can have hope that sex and intimacy will become one for me, and I can have courage to keep growing as a sexual being.

Going back to the leather bar was a big step. In my understanding of what it means to be a leatherman, the leather bar is home—no, more than home. *The leather bar is a leatherman's birthright.* Yes, it's a place to cruise and hook up but more crucially it's also a community center and, for me at least, something like a temple. It remains one of the places I am most comfortable and centered. In returning to the bar, I let the Big Book guide me. In

"Working with Others" it says "our rule is not to avoid a place where there is drinking, *if we have a legitimate reason for being there*" (101). I never just "went out" to the leather bar. I went out because I needed time in my gear, in a safe space, to reconnect with that part of me. I went out to enjoy a cigar. I went out to reconnect with leather friends, enjoy their company, and then I headed home to bed. It took a lot of "motive checking" and I wasn't always perfect about that, but I did make progress.

I remember one of my first times out at the bar. I was full of "stinkin' thinkin'," comparing myself to all the others around me and coming up real short. Before the Program that kind of thinking led to me going home, *screaming* at God about how unfair it all was. Before the Program, that kind of spiral would have usually led me to resentment and then right back to my disease. But this time, for whatever reason, I did something different—I prayed, right there in a corner of the bar. My prayer wasn't eloquent or long. I just remember asking for help. About five minutes later, my sponsor walked around the corner. It was a mutual surprise, and he looked truly relieved to see I did not have a drink in my hand. We chatted some about the relative depths of our interests in leather, but what I took away from that evening wasn't about my sponsor but it was about my Higher Power. I was learning He was there for me anytime and, more importantly, *anywhere.* I stopped believing in coincidences that night: I prayed for help, and help came. That was proof enough for me. These days I head out to the bar a couple of times each month. I gear up, get there early (10:30 p.m.), meet my friends, enjoy a cigar, and head home early too (by midnight, when the crowd starts to change). I'll say this much—I've never been more grateful to be sober than when I am watching drunks stumbling around that bar. I pray for them.

Going back online was another big step for me. It's where I had met a lot of people that had led to a lot of my using. But it's also where I had connected to leather friends around the country. This time, step one, coming to accept my own powerlessness, was my guide. Going back online I knew I had to be honest and I mean *rigorously* honest. I started by cutting out all the quick hook up and sex sites. They just didn't fit in my life anymore and they had become part of the people, places, and things I knew to avoid. Instead, I focused on sites that allowed for more conversation and chat and even then, on each one, in every profile, I stated clearly and unequivocally that I was sober and in recovery. That turned out to be an amazing part of my journey. In being honest, I met dozens of men also into kink and also in recovery. It's been an amazing way to share experience, strength, and hope.

As I've grown in my recovery I've also discovered that staying sober was the *very least* of what the program gave me. My spirituality blossomed, grew, deepened, and filled my life. Having worked the steps, I came to understand and embrace the principles behind each one. That's when I realized that the spiritual principles of the Twelve Steps are the same as many of the core values of my leather community: honesty, trust (a combination of hope and faith), courage, integrity, willingness, humility, brotherly love, service. Integrating the sober me and the leather me became very easy because of the consistency of these values. My program and my kink both became deeply spiritual practices for me.

And of all of those principles, integrity perhaps means the most to me today. A leatherman's integrity is the cornerstone of his reputation, and in the kink community that I know, reputation and respect are basic currencies. For me, a leatherman's word is his bond. If he says he's going to do something, he does it. If he can't, he lets you know. What's interesting to me, though, is that while integrity for me certainly does mean keeping my word, I'm drawn as well to the root meaning of the word, which connects it to being whole. Integrity, being integrated, integral, being whole—this is what it means for me to be a sober leatherman today. To have integrity is to be all parts of me: the sober me, the crazy me, the loving me, the awkward me, the sexy me, the scared me, the human me, the spiritual me, and yes, the leather me.

I know part of what made this entire journey of integration possible for me was the fact that I was part of a leather community before my disease really took hold. I know, too, that's not the case for many gay men and so it may not be the case for you. If you just look to porn then you won't see the community I know, nor will it stand out at a circuit party. If those have been your experiences with leather then there are some things you should know. First, and above all else, know this: *At its core, my leather community is vehemently anti-intoxication.* A good scene is not about pain or pleasure or sex or getting off but about being present, really *present*, something we can never be while messed up. The guiding principles of kink reflect this understanding: safe, sane, and consensual. For me, playing while active in my disease was *not* safe, was (by definition) insane, and obscured any possible consent. Second, the thing I forgot and have been blessed to rediscover, is that leather has enormous spiritual potential. Many religious traditions around the world have histories of rituals of pain that evoke ecstatic and divine revelation. But bracketing all that mystic and religious history (what friends of mine would call the "woo woo" stuff), I can tell you from my experience that there have been scenes where I have felt something much bigger than me moving through me. Sorry, I just don't have better words for it. I only know that my deepest spiritual moments have happened in the midst of extremely kinky leathersex. I have held men as they cried. I have watched the souls of men heal. I have been in the presence of the divine while booted, geared, gloved, and smoking a fat stogie.

This past April I taught at a local leather event. After my class, a woman came up to me. She told me that some years ago she had a stroke and since then she's had no short term memory. Then she told me the *only* thing she remembered from the event the previous year was my class, one on catharsis and healing. That's not me. That's God. In Edmonton, I taught a class on catharsis. There, I helped one of the other presenters begin to grieve the loss of a close friend. By the end of the class, the entire room was in tears. That's not me. That's God. This summer, I accidentally burned a demo-bottom, the volunteer submissive that I used for demonstration purposes. It was in a cigar sex class when some hot ash fell onto her chest. She wrote me after to tell me that she realized the burn, over her heart, connected her to the stillborn child she had cremated in April. That's God, too.

I know that my experience is not the same for some others. I know of many people in twelve-step rooms whose only experiences of leather are mixed up with alcohol or substances. For those that needed all that to overcome shame or disgust or whatever feelings they didn't want to feel, then I can tell you this: it's possible to be sober in leather. I say "possible" because I don't know what your path is. I can't say how healthy this is for you. I can only do what I am doing now: share my experience, strength, and hope.

I can also tell you too that you're not alone. Along the way I've discovered a whole community of recovering leatherfolks—and not just the ones I connected to online. I've heard of kink-specific meetings in a couple of cities, have been to one or two pansexual recovery meetings organized under "Recovery in the Life," and know that should I ever make it back to International Mister Leather in Chicago that there are meetings there every day. Today I have sober friends, leather friends, but perhaps most importantly sober leather friends. I teach at events around the country on topics ranging from bondage to impact play to catharsis. At each one, I find meetings and other sober kinksters. It's not that different from being gay: *we're everywhere*.

I'm grateful for that larger kinky, sober community because none of this has been something I've been able to discuss with my sponsors very much. My first, the one who showed up at the bar, relapsed when I had nine months; my second and current sponsor knows all about my kink life, even though he doesn't share those passions. He does share his experience, strength, and hope and when I bring anything to him he always offers some sort of guidance. Still, a lot of decisions about leather and kink I make on my own. Well, no, that's not right at all. I've made them all—still make them all—with my Higher Power.

I've sought some outside help, too. Not for the leather stuff, which is as natural to me as recovery is today, but for the more complex issues of love and intimacy and kink. My therapist has heard it all. He's also helped me see how truly consistent leather is with the rest of my life, my recovery, and my spirituality. Along the way, I've taught him a thing or two about the leather community. It doesn't hurt that I found an excellent therapist who's also in the rooms. But if you think you need outside help and fear judgment, do an Internet search for the "Kink Aware Professionals" list. There are many out there who understand and many more who won't judge.

This past March, I did a workshop on leather and sobriety at our local Round-up. We focused on negative emotions we might attach to kink and how we might have used the drink to cover those emotions. We discussed, too, the ways in which the principles of The Twelve Steps are just about the same as the values found in leather communities. Then, in June, I taught the inverse workshop at a pansexual kinky summer camp in Maryland: a workshop for "normie" leatherfolk on how to use spiritual principles like the ones in the steps. Sober? Leather? Yes.

I'm still booted and bearded at meetings. I might have my septum ring in and you'll surely see my ink. I bring some of the leather me to meetings just as I bring all of the sober me to kink. Yes, just some of the leather me. Meetings have become something almost sacred for me; they are not the place I cruise. That leather me is there because I keep thinking that someday someone's going to walk into that room for their first meeting, someone like me. And when he gets there, when he finds the solution, when he looks around, I want him to see someone who looks like him. I want him to know that who he is will change (because this is a program of change) but that here on the other side of that change there remains the possibility of leather, nasty, kinky, dirty raunchy, wonderful sex—and spirit.

That finally happened last October, when I walked out of a meeting and ran into someone I knew from parties at the local leather store. Today he's my sponsee. Last week we went to one of those parties together, sober.

I'm signing this "Edge." It's the name I use when I teach and on many of the sites I'm on. Hope to see you at an event, online, at a leather bar, at a meeting, or wherever our Higher Powers may let our paths to cross. Because this is a wonderful path—leather, sobriety, life. Do not be afraid of it.

Sobriety and Love Addiction
Chris Steele

I first went to Alcoholics Anonymous in October of 1987 at a gay A.A. group named Lambda in Dallas, Texas. I had previously been through a recovery group called Alternative Identification Ministries: Homosexual Recovery Through Christ, also called AIM. Since that was my only experience with group meetings, I decided that if A.A. were anything like AIM, I just wouldn't stay. During my first A.A. meeting I really wanted someone to mention Jesus so I could justify leaving but that never happened. At the end of the meeting a guy not much older than I was stood up and announced that he had one year of sobriety. Everyone cheered and clapped for him. I was amazed and right away I wanted what he had.

Staying sober during my first year in A.A. was difficult. I would run out of the meetings as fast as I could and sprint down the hall to the elevator so I could push the button in time to ride down alone. I didn't want to have interaction with anyone if I could avoid it. I slipped and returned to drinking on a regular basis. I usually slipped on a Friday and would return to get a new desire chip the following Monday.

There is a practice in some A.A. meetings that newcomers don't do the fourth step, the fearless and thorough personal inventory, until they have one year of sobriety. The first year is spent on steps one through three, surrendering, finding a higher power and coming to believe. Since I wasn't certain I could make it through the weekend sober, much less a year, doing the steps seemed impossible to me. I also had a big problem with meeting guys and falling desperately in love, then being hurt miserably. I would frequently become trapped in the cycle of searching for love, finding it, ruining it, hurting myself then returning to binges of sex and alcohol. I could stay sober as long as I wasn't "in love" but the minute I met someone I would fall back into drinking and self-destruction.

Against the wishes of my sponsor I sought help outside of A.A. specifically in the form of cassette tapes by co-dependency counselor Pia Mellody. I also got a lot of help from listening to tapes of Bob Earl and an A.A. speaker named Don Madden. This helped me greatly, but I couldn't avoid falling in love again. It was bound to happen sooner or later no matter what.

In November of 1988, when I was twenty-something days sober, I met a guy and fell in love. That week I was beaming from ear-to-ear in A.A. meetings. A friend of mine heard me babbling on and on about how in love I was, so he invited me to coffee after the meeting. He tried to get me to see that I was fooling myself, but I insisted he was wrong. He gave me his card and told me to call him when I got hurt, and he told me, "Because you're going to get hurt, really bad." I ignored his warning and wrote him off as jealous.

The next day I went on my first date and just like my dates had always gone before, I was promptly dumped. This guy not only dumped me, he left me in a gay bar for a girl. I was probably so crazy I drove him back to women. I can joke about it now, but when it happened I broke into tears then segued into anger followed by a high resolve to change my outward appearance. I decided that if I were blond, guys wouldn't dump me, so I drove to the twenty-four-hour grocery store in search of the right shade of hair color that would "fix" me.

As I compared prices and colors, I met another guy, the DJ from the gay bar where I had been dumped earlier that same night. I drearily told him how I was planning to bleach my hair blond, and he was so smitten with me he invited me to breakfast. Over breakfast I spilled my guts about how distraught I was over being dumped. I told him every detail except for the fact that I had only known the other guy for about four days. This new guy seemed to like me more and more with every imperfection I revealed about myself, and there was certainly plenty to like. We eventually made our way back to my apartment and we had sex, after which I found myself in a very familiar conversation, only this time it was clear that he had fallen in love with me.

Ironically, my emotional pain seemed to make me irresistible to this new guy, who was probably just as much of a love addict as I was. He broke down crying when I told him I wasn't interested in seeing him again. It was as if I were looking into a mirror of myself from earlier that night. I didn't see the emotional wall of pain building up in his eyes until he started crying just like I had done. His erratic behavior was all very familiar to me. After he left I felt like I had discovered something new about myself. I had witnessed both rejection and falling in love in a matter of hours and as a result I felt that I was cured of my need to be in love. I was certain of it. I was so sure that I decided I no longer needed to bleach my hair or otherwise change my appearance.

The next morning I replayed all the previous night's events in my head. I was still certain that because I had experienced both falling in love and having someone fall in love with me in the same night that I couldn't possibly do it again. But I was wrong. Later that night I fell back into emotional turmoil and this time the pain was much worse than I felt when I was dumped the night before. I found myself curled up on my bed crying in the fetal position. In spite of the fact that I knew how silly it was to feel so much turmoil over a guy I had known less than a week, the emotional pain seemed endless. I did what A.A. taught me to do and I got on my knees and I prayed. I asked God for an answer and it came to me. It was now midnight and something in me said the answer was with my mother. She lived fifteen miles away. I drove to my mother's house and woke her up.

A few months earlier she had gotten involved in Al-Anon, and she had already been through all twelve steps because in her group they didn't have to wait until they had one year of sobriety to do the fourth step. I told her the sad sob story about how I was dumped, and then I dumped someone, and then I had prayed for the emotional pain to end and somehow the answer to my problem was with her.

So there I was, and I needed to know, right then, why she had divorced my father when I was four years old. I needed to know about my parent's sex life. I needed to know how they met, if my father was a good lover, and all the intimate details of their relationship. She willingly answered each and every question I asked of her no matter how personal. She told me that she had been having an affair with a married man who eventually dumped her, and so she ran away to Kansas City where she met my dad, a good looking alcoholic.

I was the product of a love-addicted relationship. I was present when my parents had a major fight when I was four, and I feel like I spent many years trying to resolve the answer to the questions I was now asking my mother by playing out their relationship over and over with the emotionally unavailable men, who resembled my father, that I fell in love with.

My mom had told me about the fourth step, and how when she did it she felt like she was reaching down inside herself and opening up tin cans filled with old emotions and as she released them they turned into love and filled up her chest. As my mother answered my questions for the first time in my life, I felt my own age, I felt twenty-two. I had always felt like a little boy in a grown-up body until then.

As I stood to leave I gave her a hug and thanked her for answering all my questions. I felt taller and more at peace. I felt a calm presence, a burning sensation, in the center of my chest that made me feel whole for the first time. I now regard that warm burning calm in my chest as my self-esteem.

The fourth and fifth steps talk about how resentments affect your self-esteem, and co-dependency recovery talks about how you build boundaries to protect your self-esteem, but neither of them gives much insight or advice on how to actually build up your self-esteem in the first place.

I really didn't know what self-esteem was. I had to look up the word in the dictionary the first time I read it in the Big Book. I soon realized that in order to build my own self-esteem I had to begin to actually make decisions for myself. Up till then my self-esteem consisted of a collage of other people's ideas and suggestions about what they thought was right for me. Sometimes, I was a mosaic that could be arranged so others could see the person I thought they wanted to see. I never made decisions for myself based on what I truly wanted. I always made decisions for myself that I thought others would like. I'm not really sure why I did this except to say that I believed things that other people told me, and I let the wrong people influence my decisions for what I really wanted for myself, my esteem.

To begin building my self-esteem I started by looking at what my favorite color really was. I had always said my favorite color was green, but when I thought about it, I realized I'd chosen the color green because my childhood friend had said his favorite color was green, and so I also chose it so he would like me. Eventually the lie became the reality. Now, my favorite colors are actually black and red. Like doing an inventory, I went through my entire life and questioned my ideas, my wants, and my desires, and for every decision that affected my self-esteem I asked myself if it was something I truly wanted or was it a decision I made to please someone else. Either way the answer didn't matter. There is no way to identify the things in your own life that you like as right or wrong; the point is I had to own each and every decision because those decisions make up who I truly am.

As I made new choices for myself, I owned each of them and doing this helped to build my self-esteem. Like A.A. suggests, I threw out all of my old ideas and I let go absolutely. I made up my own mind about who I was, who I wanted to be, and what I wanted in my life. I also kept going to A.A. meetings.

I did my fourth step that November just a week after I met with my mother. I had less than thirty days of sobriety and my A.A. sponsor warned me that newcomers should wait until they have one year of sobriety before doing their fourth step. I reminded him that Ebby Thatcher had only been sober a short time when he walked A.A.'s founder Bill W. through an early version of the steps in his kitchen one morning in Akron, Ohio, and my sponsor gave me his blessing to continue with his help and guidance.

As I set out to write my fourth step, I couldn't

understand the step guides or the vague description in the Big Book, so I made up my own way to do it. I wrote down everyone I hated or wronged in grade school, starting in kindergarten and how I hated my teacher for hitting me on the ear with her pen. I went through each grade, writing down names until I reached the seventh grade, and I wrote, "I quit band because they didn't like me." I paused after I wrote that line and I looked at it. I wondered why I wrote that. I questioned if that is what I really believed, or was it some story I made up in my head to make myself feel better? I couldn't deny the sheer selfishness of that statement nor could I deny the familiarity of the pattern in my life of quitting things, especially things I really loved doing, like playing in the junior high school band.

The truth was I didn't quit band because they didn't like me. I quit band because I lost first chair when another boy showed up to band class with a shiny new trumpet his rich parents had bought him. With my school-issued brass coronet, I felt I couldn't compete with the amazing quality of his sterling silver-plated Bach. I threw a temper tantrum and the band director moved me to last chair as punishment. So I showed them. I quit.

In this listing process, I discovered I had quit a lot of things in my life. Most specifically I had quit liking or caring about myself. I discovered that I believed I was a bad person. I harbored many feelings of resentment towards myself, so I questioned where those ideas had come from. As it turned out I had allowed other people to influence what I thought of myself. I had no real reason for self-loathing or self-hatred. Like the decision that my favorite color was green, I had allowed others to influence decisions that made up who or what I thought I was.

After I finished writing my fourth step, I did my fifth step with my sponsor. I rambled on for five hours about the turmoil in my life at the age of twenty-two doing my fifth step. My sponsor struggled to stay awake, listening to every word I said, every sad story I told, every secret I revealed that I once swore no one else would ever know, and afterwards he handed me a piece of paper and told me not to read it till I got home. He explained that he had written down my eighth step list for me while he listened to my story, and he told me to go home and do step six and seven on my own then read the list he had given me. I went home and made a list of my character defects and humbly asked God to remove them all. Then I quickly jumped up and read the paper my sponsor had given me only to discover that the first name on the top of my amends list was my own.

My sponsor was right. The person I hurt the most in my life was me. So, I continued to focus on building my self-esteem, and from time to time I fell back into my old ways of searching for true love and self-destruction. Eventually I learned that I didn't have to chase guys who were not interested in me, nor did I have to judge myself by who I was in a relationship with or who I slept with. I learned how to have a good relationship with myself by deciding what was truly right for me.

At ten years of sobriety I went into the gay porn industry as a model under the name Chris Steele. I had a very successful career in gay porn, and I performed live on stage in over 100 nightclubs and venues around the world. That experience was a long way from the shy boy who used to run down the hall after meetings to catch the elevator alone. I had always been a somewhat controversial person in gay A.A. because I tended bar and managed gay nightclubs in Dallas from the time I was three years sober till my tenth year of sobriety. Most people in A.A. accepted that I was clearly going to follow my own path in life even if it included tending bar. I had some arguments with other members over my choice to support the "gay alcoholism problem" by selling it. At least that is how some members saw my choice. I usually reminded them about the passage in the Big Book that says you can't hide from alcohol. I also reminded them that I might possibly be the only representative of the Big Book that people in the gay clubs would see. Many people were not supportive and clearly did not approve of my controversial choice of employment because my job was selling liquor to my old playmates on my old playgrounds.

When I jumped from gay bars to gay porn, I stopped going to meetings at Lambda because I no longer felt welcome. Someone at the group posted a negative flyer about me doing porn on the bulletin board in the meeting hall. When I saw that, I decided that I had to be true to myself and not worry about the approval of others even if it meant not going to meetings for a while. A few years after I started in gay porn, I slowly started popping up at my old meetings to see what the climate was like.

By then I had gained some fame, and fame is a funny thing. Before having it, some people were very vocal against me and my choice to do gay porn, but once I was well known, some of these same people bragged to their friends that they knew me way back when. You need a thick skin to do porn in the first place, but to do it along with gay A.A. meetings you need it even thicker.

Even though I returned to meetings, I never stayed for the closing prayers. The moment they asked everyone to stand was my cue to exit the building and leave the parking lot. I found that if I returned to my old ways of the boy who ran down the hall to catch the elevator, then I wouldn't be cornered into justifying my choice to be a gay porn star.

There was a short time when I resented the group. During that time there was a noticeable movement in the meetings to call out anyone who didn't have a sponsor. By that time I had no sponsor, so I started raising my hand when I was in a meeting and they asked that question. I was stopped by some of my peers who, with three or more years of sobriety under their belt, asked me to stop raising my hand when the question was asked. Since I had over twelve years sober, I was setting a bad example for the newcomers. But I didn't have a sponsor and didn't like representing that I did. I didn't stop raising my hand, I just stopped going to Lambda (the gay meeting/clubhouse) again. By this time I had learned that if I stayed away from the group long enough, people would forget the issue they had with me, and when I returned, if asked, I could raise my hand to denote the fact that I do not have a sponsor. I still do not have a sponsor to this day. I believe strongly in sponsorship for newcomers but I find it difficult for people with more time, and for those of us who make a living in gay porn.

By no means am I the only gay porn star to ever be in the Program. One night I was at a meeting in San Francisco and I ran into a friend of mine who was a sober gay porn star with whom I had done an award-winning sex scene. During the meeting we slowly noticed that several people were looking our way and whispering to each other instead of listening to the speaker. There are many sober people in the gay porn industry, from models and producers to Web masters and other people who work behind the scenes. A.A. works and it works for anyone regardless of their profession.

Being a porn star did not affect my self-esteem in a negative way at all. If anything it boosted my self-esteem, because I loved the attention it brought me, especially when I was on the road stripping on stage at gay clubs. What's not to love about being a gay man on a stage with handsome, good-looking boys throwing themselves at you? I always practice the twelve steps before every live show, asking my Higher Power to keep me sober so that I may do my best to entertain the audience.

I've never lost the burning, calm feeling of self-esteem in my chest. Today I am in a healthy, loving relationship with a wonderful guy and have been for a number of years now. I have my own self-esteem that is founded on my sobriety and sustained by the discovery of who I really am. My first sponsor always told me, "You are what you do," and I accept who I am unconditionally. And as part of who I am, I have had the pleasure of standing up in an A.A. meeting to say I have another year sober twenty-two times. That is what I truly wanted to do from the very first time I came to a meeting.

Life Outside
Frank Turrentine

I have difficulty remembering what my life was like before I tried to stop drinking. There was never a long season of happy times with moments of foreboding for future troubles; I was more or less a drunk from the start. It is odd to me looking back that my folks were not more troubled by the signs I showed from an early age. They were both adult children of alcoholics; both of my grandfathers had drank themselves to death, though I was unaware of the fact until I was past adolescence.

I sometimes feel as though I spent a great deal of my adult life in reaction to some great hurt I endured, some unnamed event that set my frame of reference for everything which followed. But my childhood was fairly sheltered and comfortable. There were no instances of abuse or really anything tangible I can point to and say, "There it is." I simply never felt prepared for life. I have heard many people in meetings over the years refer to being in recovery from being raised Catholic or Baptist or the like. My response is that I was simply never raised at all. This is a lie, of course. At least, I was given the same information we all are given, about what works and what doesn't. I simply disregarded it, because I felt different. I was the baby, after all. I wasn't a brat about it; I was just everyone's favorite, the darling of the cocktail party scooting around my parents' house stealing people's highballs and enjoying the attention I got for my pre-school precociousness. My grandmother would say, "He's cute. Just ask him."

I always assumed that my family was the model for how things ought to be, but I wasn't sure what our secret was for being special. I kept waiting to feel more secure about what I wanted out of life and how I was supposed to act. It's not that I didn't know right from wrong; I just didn't know how to want to make the right choices, instead of it being an ongoing conflict. Other people made it look so easy. I wasted a great deal of time thinking there was a trick to life I didn't know. I never doubted that I was loved and cared for by my family, but I never learned basic life skills from them either. They taught me how to behave, but not how to balance a checkbook and pick up after myself. Still, as families go, I now realize I could have done much worse.

My parents split up when I was eleven. Within a year's time I got really drunk for the first time, and was already a walking casualty. Between the divorce and my difficulties with sexuality coming on, I was ripe and somewhat overdue by the time I found booze. For my first time to be actually drunk I downed the better part of a fifth of scotch after someone dared me to take a swig. I blacked out that first night, and next morning I experienced a true hangover. I felt like I had finally arrived at something that approached a solution, a muffler on the noise between my ears and a balm to the underlying sense of panic I had grown up with but could never articulate. This newly acquired habit of drinking, and it quickly and seamlessly became that, offered a sudden comfort tinged with dread, and I welcomed the change. There was a commercial for a leading antacid on television back then showing a graphic of an upset stomach with a cascade of pink liquid flowing down and the slogan, "It coats, it soothes, it protects." This is exactly the effect I experienced with alcohol. I could add, however, that it also blew up in my face about every third time and generally left me feeling like shit afterwards anyway.

My mother sent me to live with my father at seventeen. I had made the suggestion early one morning when she caught me coming home drunk, but I hadn't expected her to follow through on it so quickly. I never forgave her for that; the faded blush of that wound still colors our relationship thirty years later. She ceased to be a factor in my daily life, though she remained a presence from my past. Throughout my childhood she and I had been great companions. She had carried me with her as she went through what she called her "Diary of a Mad Housewife" phase, scribbling endless lists in steno-pads, drinking coffee, and doing crosswords on a Ouija board in her lap. She gave off a feeling of regret over choices she'd made, and she made it clear to me that she had been lied to by the men in her life. She was my advocate against my father's authority, and I was her willing co-conspirator. When my father told me she had called to suggest I move in with him, I felt like the party was over. The structure of my life did shift immediately, but the party was really just beginning. I went from the embarrassed and closeted fumblings of an adolescent queer boy in the quiet suburbs of Dallas in the 1970s to a regular at some of the very worst bars over in the city itself. I also began the pattern of relationships of dependence with the older men in my life, the set of which my father is now the only surviving member and the principal.

My father had been the vice-president of a defense company, selling things he couldn't talk about to unsavory people overseas. I thought he was James Bond, but he was really more the over-achieving only child of a couple who spent most of their time on the road in West Texas dealing with the effects of his father's alcoholism and the regular vagaries of life in the Dust Bowl and its aftermath. My father's extended family members were colorful people, alternately heavy drinkers or preachers, honky-tonk musicians or gospel singers and televangelists. They were and are clannish and insular in the way they circle the wagons about members of their group while seeking to correct their faults internally, or, at the very least, keeping the intercessory prayer going up on their behalf. No one in that part of the family has ever said a word to me about my sexuality. Rather, they focus on how I look after my father and ask if I'm going to church.

I spent my adolescence in fear of being honest with my father about my sexuality. I had great difficulty being honest with myself about it. I drank and took a great many drugs both to facilitate my desires and avoid facing them directly. In retrospect, I never wanted to change my sexuality. I simply wanted it to be OK. I felt cursed by God somehow, and I feared God. I really don't know where I picked up that bizarre Calvinist streak that I still carry, in a perverse way, now that I'm an atheist. I feared being honest. I drank at that fear. I'm sure my father suspected my sexual orientation much earlier than our conversations would indicate. But he had adopted the family method of ignoring anything that does not explode in the middle of the room. If it didn't make a mess on everyone present, it wasn't discussed. It became a fact between us before we could comfortably discuss it. It worked out the way most secrets do in my life. My behavior while drunk made it impossible to deny.

Dad had been let go from the company and opened a couple of new-and-used bookstores in the suburb where we lived. He had always wanted to have a bookstore, and it gave jobs to me, my oldest sister, and her husband for five years or so. I was a senior at a performing arts high school in downtown Dallas, where the years of piano lessons I had loathed and rarely excelled at afforded me a ticket out of the suburban hell my adolescence had become, and offered me my first experiences interacting with openly gay men my age. It was a time of great change in my circumstances, and the speed of that change only increased until life itself seemed to be moving past me, carrying the people around me, while I watched from the sidelines and drank at the missed opportunities and rapidly accumulating regrets. I began to settle in and let my father carry me along materially and emotionally while I figured out what the hell I was supposed to do with my life and hoped for some kind of windfall that would purchase my independence. I thought maturity meant being able to pay for things. I wanted control, but I was unwilling to be accountable. I was staring out at a vast unknown territory, and I didn't have a clue what to do with my life. I was seventeen, and I went to my first gay bar.

The Bayou Landing was near my high school. I had been going to bars since I was fourteen at various times; I never had much issue getting in at the places I'd been, usually topless joints up in Wichita Falls or in the rougher parts of Dallas. I went where I could get in and drink. I didn't care what the atmosphere was like, but I preferred it on the permissive side. But going to the Landing was a completely new experience. I knew that by simply being there I was letting the world in on the one part of my life I guarded most. It meant I was admitting it to myself publicly as well. No more drinking to steal vicarious thrills from other people's sexuality in topless joints. I sat down at the bar and found a hand on my knee in the space of three minutes. I was in my car with the guy five minutes later. Then I left and went home alone to my father's house.

But I had arrived in any case.

So began the regular late nights and the varying looks on my father's face the next morning when he would open my bedroom door and say with mounting frustration, "Get your friend home and get to work. You're gonna be late."

I had no intimate physical relationships. I didn't even engage in what I later heard referred to as "hostage-taking," or short-term romances. I went out drinking and wandered home with whomever and did my best to be shed of them before work the next morning. It's not like there were no models for what might work. They were few and far between, granted, but it wouldn't have occurred to me at the time to look for them in the first place. I suppose other people were forced by circumstance or the choices they made to find a different path, one that perhaps worked better for them, but this was all I was prepared for at the time. It was the '80s. Reagan was President, and everyone was on the make. I had no hustle. I had late nights and tearful mornings where I began to promise my father that I would seek some kind of help to stop drinking and get my life together. I had long, brutal mornings at the bookstore, chewing ice and sipping orange soda from the deli at the grocery store next door and sometimes lying on the dirty carpet in my father's office in back hoping the dull ache in my head would pass soon. I began to actually want help, but I feared shutting the door on my only avenue of sexual expression, oddly enough.

Two or three episodes after that last promise to my dad, I sat down one morning with the phonebook in a state of what amounted at the time to utter defeat. It was July 2, 1986. I called two or three of the treatment centers available at the time, the ones that did behavior modification with various tortures to render someone averse to the idea of drinking, but I was aware of the cost associated with having someone fix me with some sort of clinical event. The only knowledge I had at that point of A.A. was a dim memory of a woman named Mo who came to speak to my grade school when I was nine years old. I called the group listed in the phonebook and asked them how much their treatment would cost me, expecting the worst. The man on the phone chuckled and told me to come on down and have a cup of coffee.

I walked into a dimly lit, wood-paneled room in an old building; the walls yellowed by years of tobacco smoke and covered with the now familiar placards. They bore sayings such as "Easy Does It," and they reassured me in a script font vaguely reminiscent of those used in a church. An old man in khakis with a knitted kerchief secured over the hole in his throat got up from the half-dozen or so other old men and women seated at the far side of the room, shuffled into the kitchen, puffed on his cigar once, farted audibly and burped up a "goodness gracious" and poured himself a cup of coffee. I felt like I was walking into a homeless shelter, and I told myself, "Well, this is what you deserve. This is what your choices have brought you to. Suck it up and take it and maybe the heat will die down soon enough."

It worked, after a fashion, anyway. I didn't actually do anything as radical as going through the twelve-step process as it was presented to me, but I had discovered a group of people, an institution of sorts, that I thought might prevent me from screwing up so much or at least cover my ass when I next brought the house down on my head. That intuition proved to be correct in some measure over the years. I don't regret following it. At the time there was some excitement about it for me and some relief. I could lay my troubles at the feet of my "condition" and feel some sort of absolution for the tragic behavior I'd engaged in throughout my life.

I soon found my way into a gay and lesbian-oriented group over in Dallas, and my life resumed the odd bifurcation it had always exhibited around my sexuality. I see that in the passive voice even now, as though it was a structural component of my life and not a daily choice I made—to see things, to experience my very character in various parts and compartments. The last twenty-six years have been a gradual process of assembling those shattered pieces into a reasonable and coherent whole and developing a life that is authentically my own. Great chunks of that time were spent in and around or in and out of twelve-step fellowships, rehabs, religion, jails, and geographic cures or dreams of escape. I was intermittently sober, struggling, strung out, riding high, or collecting change for smokes.

Each time I slipped, I returned to the rooms and started a day count. This meant standing, telling the room of my use, and accepting a "desire chip," a white (or sometimes silver) poker chip that represented a desire to stay sober for a twenty-four-hour period. I once joked that I had enough "desire chips" to shingle a house. I had a habit of dropping them in a beer and catching them in my teeth with the last swallow.

There was a long dark period of depression in my thirties that sealed much of my past behind a wall as though encased in amber and marked a turning point in my attitudes and personality; and afterward, a gradual entrance into some sort of adulthood, an ongoing reconciliation with my past, with myself and my choices and an ongoing negotiation on how to now move forward through middle-age.

I had met the first of the old men that would help me at that little smoky group in Irving, Texas. His name was Bill Rutledge. He was a Korean War veteran, having enlisted as an alternative to a stiff prison sentence for running bootleg liquor in the Panhandle of Texas in the early '50s. He was boisterous and flirtatious with the old barflies at the Irving Group, the consummate smartass with a twinkle in his eye, a few bayonet and gunshot wounds and a lot of tragedy in his past. He was also a man of some gravity in my eyes. He was governed by a compass I lacked, and I, like some others, was drawn into his orbit. He had nicknames for me, and he was one of the old men who were at the breakfast joint at five a.m. where I would show up for pancakes and coffee every morning.

There was a point after some months in our acquaintance when Bill pulled me aside in the parking lot outside the meeting house and said, "Stewpot, what's this I hear about you not bein' a straight old country boy like I always thought?"

It was a moment I had dreaded all of my life, and it came quiet and sudden. I mustered all the courage I had and said to a man I trusted and whose acceptance I much desired, "Bill, I guess it's true, though it's not how I was raised. It's just the way I am."

"Well, my nephew is the same way. I don't understand it, but I love him, and I want him to be happy. I just wanted to say the same to you."

And with that most critical moment come and gone in an instant, I walked inside and tried to adjust to all the additional room in my life made by the great wall that had just come down. The dialogue between sexuality as activity versus identity is still ongoing, but the activity was at least no longer in another room; my life was more authentically my own. I was free of a good deal of anxiety, and I didn't realize it at the time. I did stop giggling quite so much, however.

It was at this time I met Charlie Brown. He had been sober almost ten years in the group I attended, which was a substantial period of sober time in 1986 for that

137

primarily gay and lesbian fellowship. I sat next to him at dinner after one of my first evening meetings in the group. One of the first things he said to me was, "Dear, at one time there were glory-holes in the basement bathrooms of every courthouse in Texas."

I was twenty-two, and I didn't even know what a glory-hole was until I met Charlie Brown, and the idea of Texas courthouses had always evoked images of comb-overs, cheap brown suits, and expensive cowboy boots. Sex for me was stolen blowjobs at the cockfights in Oklahoma when the other guy and I were drunk enough to pass it off later, or late night trips to the Eighth Day, a dive bar on Fitzhugh Avenue in east Dallas, to pick up whoever smiled at me near closing time. I couldn't juxtapose any of that with this stammering lavender man in poodle curls.

Charlie had polio as a child and stammered a bit as a result of that. His laugh was jarring but sincere and deep. He fidgeted, and he could be moody and overbearing to those close to him; but he responded quickly to a rebuke. He was slightly crooked, operating on the principle that there is an important difference between what is illegal and what is criminal. He would drink iced coffee and stay up all night doing office work and waiting on what we referred to as "doorbell trade." In the days before the Internet and cell phones, doorbell trade referred to tricks that just showed up and rang your doorbell.

Charlie never really challenged the notion of identity versus activity with me in almost twenty-five years. He was heavily dependent upon a routine, a rhythm dictated by his own metronome, but supporting an elaborate physical and behavioral structure created not only to sustain but to entertain. What he did teach me to do was divorce sex from sin and love and to embrace the fun of my sexuality. He also showed me a world of adult wonders that was all around me largely unobserved. I was sheltered, to say the least, wandering thirsty in a sexual desert until this little powdered sage showed me how to draw water from the rocks at my feet.

He'd been to Parson's in New York during World War II. He told stories of living at the Y, and taking servicemen to Sammy's Bowery Follies and then back to their rooms, of the colonel who kissed him on the lips at the Tiffany corner when he was seventeen, and how he never had to pay for a drink. He grew up in Dallas in a respected family with roots in the countryside south of town. His escapades as a child mirrored my own, and his candor about them shed lights into some of my darker corners. My nervous laughter dissipated even more daily. It became easier for me to relax. My periods of sobriety lengthened to many months at a time.

Charlie never had much money, but he lived such that everyone suspected there was family money lurking somewhere nearby. There was none. Charlie could dress up penury like a prince, however. He was the terror of store clerks and waiters everywhere. At the grocery store down the street they would dash for the back when he entered. When he tired of talking on the phone, with anyone, he would simply say, "OK, dear," and hang up. He did it all for free and for fun.

He also got more action than anyone I ever met. As he went about his day, as easy as dropping a pen, he was in and out of brief encounters, random liaisons in public places, guided by hieroglyphs of a secret language known only to a few and intuited by the random others, who by the alchemy of the moment are suddenly initiates into these mysteries and then once again left outside the cave with no working knowledge of its rituals. Charlie taught me that language. I can still speak it, but I have no use for it. Others fumble at it. They end their political careers in airport bathrooms and their religious careers in motel rooms. Or they end their lives tied to fences in the high plains.

There were so many other things he taught me, little things mostly. Charlie Brown gave me the nuts and bolts of how to be happy and functional, and most of all authentic. A set of wisdom put forth in sayings. My "Q Document" from the mouth of Charlie Brown, as recalled by me, from which perhaps some new gospel may someday be written:

- The capacity of the human mind for self-deception is limitless.
- Anyone can choose not only how they want to feel, but what they want to think.
- What you think about and how you feel are your own responsibilities.
- No one will ever love you or care for you exactly the way you want them to. It's not humanly possible, and besides, it's your job anyway. A corollary to this would be: If you're not willing to do it, anyone who says they want to is likely suspect.
- There is no Mr. Right. There are fifteen hundred of them. If you stand still long enough, one of them will run over you.
- Divorce your parents.
- Never deny. Never explain. In no time you'll be notorious.
- There is almost no limit to the power of permission, forgiveness, and acceptance.
- Pay yourself first.
- Spend less than you make and save the difference.
- Who loves you more than your mommy and your daddy loved you? Charlie Brown does.

All of these, of course, were delivered as dialogue between the suffering servant and the supposedly anonymous author. But Charlie, true to his own wisdom, was much too infamous to ever be anonymous.

I came to Charlie repeatedly over the years after one or another of my various watershed moments. He was the midwife of several rebirths, and he did it with the lightest of touches. He never financed my schemes or bailed me out of a disaster, but he offered me his unqualified support in just about anything I ventured. He assured me many times that I was one of those people who are more interesting to watch than they are socially profitable to know. He doted on me. He enjoyed my company because I was well read and usually willing to join him, day or night, in just about any excursion. He was Auntie Mame, Yoda, and the perfect counterpoint to the martial rhythm I grew up with. I was his partner in crime, and he was a true and loyal friend to me.

On April 1, 2006, in the late afternoon I was out in the garden tilling and daydreaming when my father walked out and offered to buy me a six-pack of beer. That's about all I had going on at the time in my life. I allowed as how that was nice of him, and I said I'd run to the beer store and come right back. I had returned from six years in Minneapolis a month earlier and settled into a daily drinking routine. The first of my adult long-term relationships had come to an end, and I was wallowing a bit.

"No," he said, "I'll ride with you."

I was forty-two years old, and I was struck by the fact that my father didn't trust me to go to the beer store and make it back with any predictability. I was overcome with this sudden realization that the only way I'd ever been able to survive the way I had was to make myself my father's pet and allow him to tend to my needs and bail me out when I made a mess of things. We had both become so accustomed to this reality that it seemed almost normal to both of us. I had constructed elaborate rationalizations for the course my life had taken. Most of the time I simply didn't think about the reality of it.

I went inside and poured out the two beers that were in the refrigerator and changed clothes and went to a meeting in the little town of Weatherford, not far from the farm. It was a Saturday night, and there were about five old women sitting around the table. I recognized some of them, though it had been years since I had been there. I told them that I didn't believe this would work for me anymore, but that I didn't know what else to do. I stuck around.

Three or four days passed, and I began to feel better about it. I decided to drive into Dallas and return to a meeting at Lambda, where Charlie and I had spent so much time in years past. Years ago I had told myself I wouldn't go back there, that there was no point in making the attempt to get sober again. But I was surprised to learn there was no bad feeling when I showed up there. I felt right at home. I began to drive over several times a week, even telling my dad that I was going to Weatherford and then heading to Dallas, an eighty-mile trip, to hit a meeting there. I was beginning to feel a certain degree of expectation about my life that I hadn't experienced in quite some time.

I asked a few people if they would work with me as a sponsor, but I was turned down for one reason or another. For twenty years, I had come in and out, usually accruing a few months or even a couple of years of dry time at most before devolving into a puddle of self-destruction and bitterness once again. I had become the bad example, the person people pointed to as a warning. That's no joke.

I finally asked George S. if he would sponsor me. George didn't say yes, but he said I should meet with him at his home for a talk. I had known George since my early days with the group. He had been sober for decades, and he had been the treatment director at one of the facilities I'd been sent to by the courts back in the '90s. I trusted him completely, but I still wasn't sure if I would be able to remain sober and become useful in any real sense. We weren't close, but we had maintained a nodding, friendly acquaintance over the years, and we both knew quite a bit about each other. I talked to him about what my life was like, and I began to fall apart. That lasted an hour or so. He gave me some writing assignments and suggested we meet again in a week.

I continued to meet with George on a weekly basis for over a year. During that time he did what no other person had ever done for me, and something for which I will be eternally grateful. He took me all the way through The Twelve Steps of that process and gave me something I had never experienced before. Hope. Perhaps anyone could have done that, since my willingness was the trigger that made everything possible. But no one could have done it the way that George did.

I wrote letters and approached people in person to make amends. I began to pay off old debts, and I did extensive inventory of my relationships and began to develop new ways of behaving toward people in my life so that I could hopefully make right at least some of the damage I had created over the years.

I was beginning to feel true freedom from the tyranny of my impulses and emotional states, and I was becoming a co-creator in my own life with the order and organization of the universe. There developed a rhythm to my life that was sustaining, even when, as George would put it, I was "stirring up dust bunnies in my head." I had an Intercessor of sorts, and I began to experience real peace of mind.

I had moved away from my father and gone back to work at a company that had employed me back in the '90s. I had gotten a place of my own and given my father back his gas card. I stopped taking money from him without paying it back. I was self-supporting through my own efforts. I made it to a year and began to sponsor other people myself. I really felt like I had something worthwhile to transmit to others for the first time in my life, and I fully expected not only my material circumstances, but my mind and behavior, to continue to improve with time. I was handed difficulties and felt no panic or need to run from them.

Toward the end of 2007, I began to experience some of the same old troubles that had afflicted me in the past. I was a bit scattered and casting about for a fix. I was encountering trouble from the same defects of character that had dogged me for years and years. This is nothing new, and I bided my time and figured some more work with George would help. Things were good, in spite of my misgivings about what lay ahead.

I talked to George about sitting down again and talking. We made plans to do that soon. All was well. George was not only a very spiritual man, he was also a trained therapist with years of experience in treating addiction. More importantly, he was my friend and had the ability to tether me back down to earth when I was spiraling off into orbit mentally. He would ignore my intellectual acrobatics and stay on point. Just knowing he was there was a great help, though I usually took it for granted.

George was kidnapped and murdered by a man he knew casually in early February 2008. I knew enough about George to appreciate the costs of his own risk-taking. There is much about the details of the crime that remains a mystery for most who knew him. But I am relatively certain that of the handful of men with whom George had worked closely over the years, I am not the only one who has spent some time writing the script of that episode with some intuitive accuracy in my mind.

For a couple of weeks, including his disappearance, the discovery of his body, and capture of his killer, the various friends flying in from out of town and the eventual funeral, everything was rather suspended, and I was numb. All of us with whom George had worked gathered together and talked about his effect on our lives and how we should stay in touch and support one another, and we meant it at the time. But we were burnt out by the emotional rollercoaster of that period of time, and we have since retreated into our various corners and kept mostly to ourselves.

I went off the reservation for several months, scattered and spinning my wheels. I still did those things that I'd always done to sustain me, but I remained somewhat at a loss. There was no substance to my rituals. I still woke every morning, turned on the coffeepot, pissed and brushed my teeth, made my bed, and got down on my knees and prayed. I then took a handful of pills for my heart and poured a cup of coffee and went into my study to write and read and meditate. I still gave thanks every night and inquired what I may do to correct my errors, and I did that sincerely. I still met with other people like myself, though not as frequently as perhaps I should have, and I still stayed in constant contact over the phone with friends who shared that same road. I told the one remaining person I sponsored that I was trying to fire myself from that job, and he said he wouldn't let me. I wasn't getting into drama. I just felt like I had very little to offer him. However, once we began to work on his list of amends I freely shared my experience, and we worked out a process for him to address those people and situations going forward. I was glad he had shown up, even though my phone was turned off and I was offline.

I eventually drank again. I spent a few months distracting myself, manufacturing romances, or doing whatever I could to stay interested in what my life had become. I wasn't terribly unhappy, but I was no longer invested in the process or the fellowship surrounding it. I wasn't bitter. I felt no burning resentments. My life had some structure to it, and I had things that interested me, but I felt as though I had placed myself outside of what I had known as the recovery community for all of my adult life. The group to which I belonged had long since lost that entire stratum of men I had known whose lives had winked out in the closing years of the last century. All that really remained was Charlie and my father. And me going forward somehow, as Charlie seemed to be on the way out.

Charlie had been a member of the Hemlock Society. I used to joke with him that he had to let me know when it was time, so I could come by and borrow a bunch of money the week before; but he had outlived the lawyer and doctor who had tacit understandings with him in that regard. So he lingered and faded and experienced intermittent days of good feeling and activity in this period long past any Indian summer of his life. No more doorbell trade or caffeine, and he had to sneak cigarettes at the assisted living center. He called every few days over the last few weeks, usually to tell me that we needed to sit down and talk about money. He was tired of us both being broke all the time, and he had an idea. I assumed he wanted me to sell pain pills or something along those lines that would amount to no profit on my end. I said I'd come by. I made excuses. I ignored calls. It's the sort of thing I've done with him for years. And then I got a text from a mutual acquaintance saying that Charlie had just died.

I drove over to his place, and he was there on the floor where he'd died. He had donated his body to the University, and they were slow in arriving. There was nothing particularly dramatic or even sad about the scene. I was certainly sad, and I felt the loss. His entrance into my life marked the beginning of a structural shift in my entire thinking. His passing was so gradual as to be almost unnoticed by most. Most of those who would feel his absence most acutely had already passed long ago. I wept a bit, gathered a few pictures and shut the door.

I thought I had made peace with my demons, such as they were. My choices were tempered by age, though I still periodically felt the pull of the sweet music playing across town. I had negotiated a space in my life for drinking and weed that largely stayed within its bounds. That may have created damaging effects on my health or impeded my functionality at times. But there was a structure to my life and other impulses that governed me besides my appetites. I felt as though I had stopped seeking oblivion and found ease. These changes did not come as epiphanies. There was little drama in my life in the last few years since George was murdered. I was self-supporting, and I had regained something of that locus of control he had wished for me. That was the rationale I created in the wake of losing George and Charlie. In twelve-step circles folks would call it "controlled drinking," and I suppose they would be correct. It was an attenuation of what was possible for me, a happiness of my own devising under whatever Grace I felt was sufficient for me.

My father still lived out on the farm eighty miles west of Dallas. I traveled out to check on him every other day and on weekends and eventually spent every night out there, waking at four every morning to make the long commute into Dallas for work. I gardened and planted trees under Dad's direction; we consider tree-planting an act of faith for both of us. I no longer tried to maintain sobriety, though my using was largely confined to sitting around the house smoking weed, listening to music, and drinking beer until bedtime, a few nights each week. I had little taste for bars and none for nightclubs. I was too engaged by other, seemingly larger questions in my life at the time for the headache and clouded thinking of a morning after to seem a tragedy for me. The underlying panic of my youth was absent, but the noise between my ears, that indefinable *thing* that drove my drinking obsession for decades was still identifiably *there* in some measure. It seemed that just like I was told there is no cure for it, and there is very little I can do to control it.

The inner-dialogue between identity versus activity as it applies to my sexuality may also have a parallel respecting my relationship with alcohol and drugs and the effect they have had in my life and how they define the way I see myself. That conundrum may never work itself out completely, but I was much less interested in answers and absolutes at forty-eight than I was at twenty-two. The hope I gained working with George was replaced by something of an ongoing engagement with life as it remained for me. To the extent that my focus remained upon those things in my life that engaged my intellect, emotions, and will—I seemed less troubled by the demons of my idle hours. I maintained many of the acquaintances I developed over a quarter century in recovery, but mostly online and in correspondence. I had nothing to argue with that fellowship of people; I also had nothing to preach at them. I did not think in terms of whether I was sober or not, though I supposed a change in circumstances, material or emotional, such as the loss of my job, getting arrested, or the death of my father might return me to that paradigm. I somehow doubted it at that point, however.

There were things I wanted to do with the time I had left. And while I maintained that I was an atheist, I believed I had been given the Grace sufficient to continue.

That is how I felt when I wrecked my truck and spent the night in jail and realized that, in spite of all the intellectual and emotional acrobatics, all the Byzantine spiritual calculus I had created to make God jump through the hoop for me and allow me to negotiate one small corner of life for myself and call it happiness, I was still an alcoholic. I will never be able to drink without running the risk of serious consequences developing as a result. The combination of alcohol and insufficient sleep had me nodding at the wheel, and I tagged a semi-tractor parked on the exit ramp of the freeway. Such an insignificant thing it seems in retrospect, the driver of the semi was able to drive off before the wrecker showed up to tow away my truck, and yet so devastating and life-changing for me at the time. And, finally, exactly what I needed; a seamless fit in the chain of circumstance that continues to progress in my life. A state trooper arrived at the same time as the friend I had phoned to come get me and my dog. My truck was a total loss.

I was handcuffed for the first time in many years, and I became a spectator for the rest of that night as I was carried to the county jail and booked. I made the calls and arrangements and got word to my father what had happened. The man I had rearranged my life to help once again became the man who picked me up from jail. We re-played a vaguely familiar act from our past, and all I felt was a deep sense of shame. At forty-eight I was beginning the re-enactment of a scene I'd thought long finished, a struggle long ago completed and put away.

I returned to the twelve-step group I had so long been a part of a few days after I got out of jail, and I once again established a start in that process. I was too caught up in the consequences of the wreck and my pending legal troubles to worry much about what people would think or where I now fit in that fellowship. My circumstances were too scattered, the details of my life too chaotic and beyond my control, for me to worry about how things looked to other people at the moment. Even after an absence of more than three years the routines were easy to pick up, the structure of that life an easy fit. But the questions for me going forward were daunting. I asked someone I knew who had, like me, worked with George for many years if he would work with me as a sponsor, and he agreed. I told him that for the first time in my life I honestly considered cutting my own throat. He said that was off the table of options, and I consented to forego that and see things through no matter what.

The process as I had worked through it with George had been pretty exhaustive and complete at the time, and there had been little added during my absence that required its repetition. But I did sit down with my friend and share some of the big secrets I had previously shared with George and the truths about myself that I had gleaned from that. He gave me a few simple things to do on a daily basis and encouraged me to call him regularly. Since that time I have pretty faithfully adhered to that prescription. I returned to looking after my dad and gardening and making the long commute every day for work with the addition of meetings with the group, usually at lunchtime in the city. I begin and end my days with a simple prayer and a reflection on the day's events with an eye toward resolution of my angers, fears, resentments, and dishonesty. I read a little from the literature of recovery, and I look for ways that I can be of service, though my circumstances limit that mostly to how I can be helpful to my father. There are large, looming legal questions that remain unanswered, and I fear the results, but I ask forgiveness for those fears and ask that they be removed and try to substitute another thought in their place when they arise. There is resentment toward my father, my boss, my friends, institutions, and ideas that come up during the day, but I generally recognize them for what they are, unproductive of anything but unhappiness and discord, and I work toward their removal.

There is no great joy in my life at present, but my troubles are of a manageable size when taken daily and referred and refracted through this process of ongoing recovery. I hear stories from others of troubles surmounted and put to rest, and I have some measure of hope that I will live through all of this and that my attitude toward my circumstances will change. That doesn't perhaps sound like much, but it is a world of difference from where I was in the days following my arrest. Perhaps I no longer believe in miracles, but I believe in a sustaining Grace that will carry me through whatever lies ahead on a daily basis. I have been given the necessary willingness to do whatever is in front of me and not fear the consequences, so long as I remain a person who is accountable. I would, however, welcome a miracle. In lieu of that I will continue in faith, trusting that this process I have once again given myself up to will provide whatever I need on a daily basis to carry me through whatever circumstances I helped create with the choices I made that got me here.

I have learned a great deal from all the old men in my life over the years. The one lesson I continued to disregard and reject was that one plain truth about me; I cannot drink like normal people or use drugs recreationally. It is the one true thing that always stood in the way of my chance of having an authentic life of my own, so long as I ignored it or refused to accept it as true. The basis of any possible happiness is grounded in that acceptance, and no loss, no circumstance will negate that for me. It is, finally, the marriage of activity with identity in my life, the end of that bifurcation in my character, which is the call I always refused and avoided. I am a gay man, and I am an alcoholic. These are not things that I do, but part and parcel of who I am. I cannot segregate and compartmentalize those facets of my character without risking my integrity and my identity. The path to happiness for me somehow lies through that truth I have avoided. More, as they say, will be revealed, but it is a good place to start and a good place to be after all these years.

For Gay Boys Who Want to Try Meth
Peter Joshua

My life—at least the time I spent as a crystal meth addict—can be plotted as precisely as a graph. It has a very definite start and end date. On paper it would look more like a stock offering– opening high, then receding after the initial wave of euphoria and then gathering strength over the years until it goes bankrupt, or is taken private. Like most graphs, it doesn't really tell the full story. Even numbers can be manipulated to tell the story you want to tell. As it turns out, so can most addictions if you live long enough to tell the tale. That's one of the reasons I didn't clean up by going to A.A. or another version of a twelve-step program. I'm a writer, I know too much about how to tell a story. Stories are often memories—and memories are infused with time and with lies, both true and untrue.

As soon as the drug found me, I knew I was in trouble. And I knew I could never have it again. That was clear. It never occurred to me to go to A.A. I'd known very few who had ever come out of A.A. sober, and by sober I mean really sober. The people I did know seemed to trade one addiction for another. The ones I knew and liked, I put into a category I'd put myself in: they had reached a natural end where stopping had more to do with a common natural truth—this drug is killing me. I don't want to die this way. This was sordid and disgusting, and worse, the drug wasn't even getting me what I thought it delivered—a mythical, universal ability to be open, relaxed, fun, and charismatic with an astonishing sex drive. If there's one slogan I'm fond of now it's, "So you take meth. Your breath smells, your teeth rot, your jaw clenches, you can't come, it takes a week to recover, and you die? Great. Sign me up."

Looking back, if anyone had got me to A.A., I know I wouldn't have told the truth. I'm not sure that I could have admitted that I could get so dependent on something I could clearly see didn't end well. I'd have told some form of the truth.

In the end, some hard financial knocks, age, friends, and a great therapist, combined with luck, were enough for me to kick meth. That is the truth. Except of course for all the other things I'm leaving out. Like the real truth, the stuff that made getting off meth the easy part.

It was Lillian Hellman, a tough-drinking, hard-living lady if ever there was one, who used the word *pentimento* as the title for a memoir. Pentimento means literally to repent, or change one's mind. In some old paintings, the paint fades so centuries later you can sometimes see a tree underneath a church, or the line of a person that might have been.

"The paint has aged now and I wanted to see what was there for me once and what was there for me now," Hellman writes, or words to that effect.

Lillian was telling it like it is. All any of us can do is tell the truth as best we know it. I changed my mind about crystal meth. There's much about my journey to it and away from it that will remain with me until I die. That's like A.A. I never understood what people meant when they said they were recovering alcoholics, that you had to say, "I'm an alcoholic." Now I know, in part, what they mean. Now I'm more or less constantly aware of the struggle to resist doing a line, or putting your house or child on the roulette table simply because you can't face— or don't even know—what is really bothering at the root of the problem.

The start is the start. I knew nothing about meth. I'd never even heard of it.

All I know is that I was at a party that started on a Friday evening in May and by Sunday morning I was a sexual God, prized not just for my stamina and prowess but also for an erection that wouldn't stop. And that every once in a while there was a bitter tingling on my lips and eventually a little pinch on my ass as someone put it right into my asshole. Why ask what it is when you're having so much fun?

Amazing things happened at that party. There was a handsome man who I'd urged on like a midwife to take his first fist. Not that I really knew what that was—I wasn't the person fisting, I was the *eminence gris*, his connection to the world of pleasure. My job was to help him open up, let go, and get him to the other side. And I was sensationally good at it. I was invested with someone's soul to help them get somewhere they didn't think they could go. And they got there. And he loved me for it. He told me so. Over and over.

It's where we all want to go, right? That line between the true and the untrue. The subtle deadly space between good art and great.

Whatever I was doing with that boy in the sling felt like that—transportation out of yourself to a land of beauty and pleasure. And I wanted in.

And it was then that the party turned on me.

I'd had my fun and the group was determined that it was my turn. They'd been feeding me those drugs with intent, and now it was payback time for the innocent one who assisted so well. There's nothing quite like fresh meat at a meth party. Cocks, unlikely, toys possibly, fists certainly. It was my time in the sling. I wasn't ready. And I was scared.

I escaped out of the dark playroom to rest.

Anyone who has ever been to a meth party knows that what got me out of this predicament wasn't my rediscovered morality. I was just at the end of the line and everyone is relieved when the guy who has been fucking them doesn't want anything in return. It had the slight effect of burnishing my reputation as a true top—a skill that would help (or hurt) later on.

In that next room, the first shock was discovering with the grey first light of morning that two days had gone by instead of a few hours. And that the chemical that had made this happen wasn't great coke as I'd assumed—but crystal meth. That little tingle in my hole was called a booty bump and I'd had many of them. And then the real kicker: I had a few hours to get to work.

And not just work—I was the host of an awards ceremony that started in less than twenty-four hours and there was a rehearsal in eight hours. Skipping work was out of the question. Standing in a stranger's apartment trembling uncontrollably and stinking of sweat and lube and every bodily fluid, I had to make some serious decisions.

My Australian host that weekend is the first of many who I have to thank for the fact that I survived meth.

"You'll never make it. You have to cancel," my host said. "You're going to be up for the next two days. You'll be really speedy on Monday, miserable on Tuesday, and you might be presentable on Wednesday."

I don't remember what I said. I don't remember if I told him who I was, or what I had to do—it doesn't matter. He got it.

"Oh my God. You really are a virgin." And I suppose, in a way, I was.

He handed me two Ambien, four Valium, a bag full of Gatorade, and sent me home with dark sunglasses and instructions to close all the blinds, watch old movies, and not to jerk off.

"You won't come and you'll pull your dick off. Just don't do it."

I didn't believe him. I did believe that I was in serious trouble.

"If you keep chugging liquids, and get some sleep, you might make it through the next few days," the Australian told me. "And if you do get through this, never do it again. You're not the right type for this drug. I know you think you are, but you're not."

I wasn't convinced he was right about my being the right or wrong type—we'd leave that to the future. I just had to get through the next few days.

And I did make it through the next two days. And I did come.

For me it has always been about winning.

Everything I'd watched in movies or read about drug addiction was coming true. What did I do that night? What did I say? I know I went to that rehearsal.

And work the next day.

And at the awards the next evening, in black tie with my tall, sequined ex-girlfriend chosen to play the role I'd imagined for myself that night—poised, famous writer with politically astute, socially on cue female love interest. I wanted us to look like the new power couple. Did she know? Could she smell the faint aroma of vegetable shortening over the ounces of cologne? She knew me so well, or was it all just so glamorous that she didn't notice? One day I must ask her. I was onstage for the world to see. Television cameras whirred, pictures on red carpets and bright lights. All eyes were on me, and yet I knew they weren't. Or were they?

Did I talk too much? I was quite sure I was speaking at the speed of light. Could they see me sweating? The speedy bit of the comedown was happening on cue.

I think then as I think now—probably yes. And probably no.

And I got one of the top awards that night.

What a shame I really wasn't there to accept it.

Everyone else went off to celebration parties, and I went home to bed like Eve Harrington too cranky to attend her own party.

No matter. The combination of amazing sex, a drug that nearly cost me my career, and a lost week of my life had convinced me that my friend was right. Meth was not for me.

When I was sixteen, a smart, sexy older woman I was playing with took a line of coke right out from under my nose. All the tough guys we were hanging around with protested. "C'mon, let him play, he's a grown up."

I wasn't. I'd lied about my age to get the job. I was passably twenty-one.

"You're the wrong type for this drug," she whispered and then led me by the hand off to a pine glen by a lake where we made love all afternoon.

Thank you, Joanna. She kept me sober far longer than the Australian did.

I had dinner with my Australian savior not long after I'd recovered. My brush with destruction kept me away from the drug. It didn't keep me away from the Australian. I needed to talk to him. I needed to understand how to get back to that dark, heavenly room without the very unpleasant side effects and into the sling to have my chance at learning to let go. I asked him if it was possible to do all that we did that party weekend without the drugs.

"Why would you want to?" he responded.

Why, indeed.

We were at a new restaurant and people kept stopping by to say hello. My friend would pass in and out of sleep. He was alternately pale and sweaty and chatty. It was getting so obvious that he was wacked out that I asked the restaurant staff to help me get him off the banquette and into a taxi. The bright lights of New York City are no place for the crystal meth people. We live in the dark.

And all this time I was in therapy. I didn't share a word of these experiences with my therapist. There was enough to talk about. I was learning, if nothing else, that a compulsion towards constant sex has nothing, or at least very little, to do with sex at all. "Sex isn't really sex," she'd say.

What is it?

Running away from loneliness?

Running away from your desk?

I justified.

What artist doesn't have The Problem? Alcohol? Sex? Drugs? Depression?

The end of phase one merely foretold that I was in a lot of trouble, but that trouble wasn't with crystal meth.

Fate also intervened. A dead parent. A book to write. A move to the country to write the book.

It was in the country that I met meth again.

It was also here that I met, not for the first time in my life, "The Program." I'd accompanied friends in A.A. to meetings. I'd gone to Al-Anon meetings. I even went to a few N.A. meetings. Not, you understand, because I was taking meth. I wasn't using. I would have regular weekly dinners at my home for friends who were in recovery. I was their safe spot. The one person they knew who was sober.

Always the *eminence gris* and so very comfortable in the role.

From the earliest age I was the person who took care of people. It's my special gift as it is to so many children of artists, alcoholics, depressives, and suicide cases. There can't be anyone—or at least very few in the world better equipped to deal with someone else who is going through the consequences of addiction.

It's what I'm trained for.

It's just that no one is allowed to take care of me. That's the rule.

None of them knew that I was just as addicted—my addiction was just back there somewhere at that party, and in the years before it.

I wanted to experience letting go to the point of addiction. In my head it looks like (and feels like) a ski jump—the moment you let go, you set down the slope and then there is a moment of no return when you take off and fly off into the air—the release, the quiet, and then the pinpoint landing. It's not the landing that has ever scared me. It's the point where you takeoff. Where there's no return. Like the moment when they drop the blade or pull the lever. I've always believed I know what that feeling would be like. In that space though, is where all the magic is.

Writing is just like that. You have to walk up the stairs and you have to let go for it to be good. And you may die in the process.

Sitting down to write is hard.

Getting sex on the Internet is easy. And it's not scary at all.

That's what brought me back to meth.

It turns out my friends in recovery (many of whom fell off the wagon later) taught me much. Mostly they kept me on track. I wrote and published my book. And at the end of my first book party I was dining with people I didn't know. By the second, I was on the road, in strange cities, avoiding the book parties and seeking sex wherever I could find it. When the first meth pipe touched my mouth it never crossed my mind to say no. The next part of my wave had begun.

I laugh when people say meth is a drug for the poor. My mind reels back to the parties I'd spent with the sons of billionaires calling in for their stashes from the Bentley. The musicians and intellectuals and writers like me who thought we were so clever to live in this strangely anonymous world. It was a world of apartments that had slings that dropped from a ceiling with the touch of a button, or cages that rose up from the floor, hot tubs on rooftops, rooms of sex toys and leather outfits, projection booths of porn that were like DJ booths filled with DVDs by the hundreds, all covered with sticky fingerprints.

These were lives that somehow money protected.

I rather came to think that meth was a privilege of the very rich, or at least the rich enough.

That's what made it OK.

That's what made it not an addiction.

We were smarter than that. None of us were going to let a recreational party drug take us down. And the depravity of it kept us out of the newspapers. Who would ever believe people like us would enjoy such deliciously dark things?

Don't worry. Meth does wreak its way through almost every checkbook and takes no prisoners anyway. For every loft penthouse there was also a highway rest stop at five a.m. Brushes with the law were always just one or two steps away. There were the secret basement flats that had been condemned, literally, not that their owners ever claimed to be as chic as Studio 54. Though I do often wonder if the famous cage at 54 was just as depraved as the basement cages I saw. For every hotel suite (that I paid for) filled with drugged-up porn stars, where I fucked for days, there were as many people who could barely move through their filth. For all the times I managed to get up and go work out, there were the physical feats that made me understand why William Burroughs shot his wife in a drugged up game of William Tell. There were morning benders that had me in motels at nine a.m. willing to do almost anything—and I did.

People I'd spent aimless hours with one day before, their houses or apartments always in some state of mid-construction, were dead the next day. Or in prison.

I never thought of A.A. Not once. I took other people to A.A.

"Let it out, we've heard it all," I remember hearing at one meeting.

No, actually, you haven't heard it all. And what I have to say I don't want to share with a group. Not with any of you. It's my job to take care of you.

How can you say to someone—to a group—that you went through all of that and still, come the morning you were the only one who still couldn't let someone fist you? At the moment anyone tried, at the moment when all this attention was finally on me, I couldn't let anyone in, literally or figuratively. My visceral, instinctual fear was stronger than the drug.

And yet, pentimento. There were a few people who could see behind the surface when they looked into my eyes. A few who said, "I will take you there if you want me to. Head down the slope. At the moment of your greatest fear, we have to trust each other." Still, every time, just at the point of lift off at the very bottom of the ramp, I'd scream to make them stop. They listened. Those are the ones that lived. Those are the ones that made it worth it. Those are the guys I later found out were sober guys.

They are the ones who, in time, would lead me out and to whom I would tell the truth. I remember one saying, "If you like doing this, might I suggest that doing it without is evening better?"

At one stage my friend John and I decided to buy a house together. He was someone I'd met, and we'd thought we'd build a splendid retreat for all the parties we'd enjoy while we got older and had more time to spend on weekends. I sold my apartment in the city and moved in with John and his boyfriend. I didn't think of it that way, but I'd already smoked my next advance away. No matter. It occurred to me that perhaps the decision to continue to build a new house with John wasn't made while I was thinking clearly, but not enough for me to say no.

Something was beginning to stir in me. Was I a little bit in love? Or was it the drug? Or was I just the *eminence gris* again? Now I know he did love me. We protected each other, and he protected me from my future creditors.

I'd never had a roommate outside of college before. And it seemed this kept us both safe. Or made the end look farther away.

Years passed. One weekend I took my ex-wife and son to see the Barnes Collection in the leafy suburbs of Philadelphia. We laughed and played and had adventures we recount to this day.

On the train ride back, my son came up with the idea that we should all travel to some city on Amtrak every month. So we could all be together, so we could be a family. He'd pick the city.

As I watched his happy face, I had to explain, gently, that I couldn't promise every month. You see, I'd already put weekends aside for sex parties and built in mandatory recovery time into my life. I'd become a functional addict.

When I got back to the city a few hours later, my roommates were having an old fashioned cocktail party, nibbles in bowls and martini shakers shaking. I might have been projecting but I sensed a certain distance from all the guests. The clink of glasses, the laughter of people I didn't know in an apartment full of stunning antiques that weren't mine felt hollow for the first time.

I walked into my bedroom.

Laid out on the bed on top of my princely ironed sheets was my collection of dildos. They were all sparkling clean, all in a tidy line and all very visible to anyone who walked by to use the bathroom.

I let out an uncontrolled scream, "Is there NO privacy? Does ANYONE care that I live here?"

There was no answer. No one was listening.

It turns out John's misunderstood boyfriend must have spent the weekend faintly smelling the detritus of some session the week before and pulled out from under my bed the filthy toys we hadn't cleaned and created a display for my humiliation.

John didn't come to my rescue. I was on my own. I was the drugged-up, untidy, sex pig who had just sold another block of his inheritance to pay for his next shipment of meth.

I closed the door. I seethed. I listened to the chatter next door and vanished into what amounted to a nervous breakdown. Spinning through my head were these thoughts: I'd sold my apartment, I'd borrowed a million I couldn't pay back, I'd imperiled my career, I'd lied to my child, my family, my friends, and myself. I didn't even have a closet of my own. No place to hide my secrets anymore. Worse—I'd hardly written a word since my last book and I was still as closed up, as unable to trust and as alone as I had ever been.

The physical manifestation of this was that I thought I was having a heart attack and yet I couldn't move. I made it through the night, barely, and went to the doctor the next the morning. I didn't say, "I've come to admit that I have a drug problem." I went because I knew I was having a much more serious problem. I was out of control emotionally, physically, and financially.

My doctor cupped my head in his hands. I flinched.

Here's me, a person longing to get fisted by strange men but who reels at the touch of someone whose help I'm seeking.

"We can fix this," he said. I tried to cry but I couldn't. It felt good enough just to let the weight of my head rest in his hands. I did not tell him I had trouble with crystal meth. I didn't need to. This was my step one.

He prescribed a series of mild anti-depressants and something to calm me down.

Then, I went back to therapy, which I'd left many years earlier after my therapist had tried to put me into a group. We got into a fight about why. She thought groups were petri dishes where the whole told a story. In the early years of one-on-one therapy I'd learned, or thought I'd learned, that I am allowed to say "no." I was finally saying "no" to group. She persuaded me to do it anyway and with disastrous consequences. I got sucked into the lives of everyone in the group. And she unintentionally mocked me when I failed. We parted company on this issue well before my meth years. But I came back for long stretches during them—making sure my sessions were always on Thursdays.

She was the first person I needed to tell.

It came out easier than I thought.

"Many of the years I was in therapy with you I never told you that I had a drug problem. Did you know?"

"I had wanted to ask...."

"That's an evasive answer," I said.

"No," she said in that calming voice she used to call "speaking to my brain." "I knew you'd lie. I knew you'd think drugs were the problem, not the sex—not the need to take care or think you have to take care of everyone. That's what you do. That's your addiction. You're trained to fix everything and everyone, but not yourself."

This was a good start. She wasn't angry at me.

"Can you stop doing crystal today?" she asked.

"No problem," I said. "Do you think I should go to A.A.?"

"Do you?"

"No."

"Why?"

Long pause. "You know I hate groups. I can't do it."

"Yes, you do. I was wrong to try to put you in group. It wasn't right for you then and it's not right for you now. I should have apologized then. I am apologizing now."

I burst into tears.

I cried for a long time. *Ordinary People* stuff.

She never held me, and she didn't then.

I didn't need her to.

"What will you do now?"

I just stopped. I went and took myself off every sex site everywhere in the world I'd sought sex out. Eventually, I stopped thinking of every moment of every day as a way towards sex. I dumped what drugs I had down the toilet. Later, not so long after I was really sure, I took the pipes and paraphernalia and crushed them in the street. And not long after that I started to reach out to the people I thought might have survived.

It was to them that I wanted to say, "I was on meth when I made that decision," not to any group. I wanted to say this to John, who after I moved out was no longer dependent on me financially. I'll be there for him when he needs me. Or not.

Trying not to judge is an important part of my cure. I wasn't honest with myself when I was on meth, why should anyone else be?

I went back on my own, where I belonged, and found other pieces of my cure.

The ones who are dead, and there are many, I remember.

The ones who lived, and who, like me, could admit meth wasn't something within our control, I keep very dear to my heart. For those who I think I love or loved then, I tell them to call me when they get sober.

The ones who had nothing to do with my using but guessed that I knew a little bit more about the underworld of sex and drugs than I cared to admit, I told them.

The ones who are still using, who occasionally reach out, I do my best to let them know that I'm sober.

The main thing is I don't offer to be their sponsors, fix their lives, or let them move in or build them homes. I don't need to take care of everyone. I can say "no."

Tell yourself the truth first and the rest will follow.

I told my best friend, who had had a not dissimilar experience with alcohol and got off it the same way I got off meth. Our lives were both too public and too private to deal with groups. We'd done almost everything the same way since we were kids and in some ways, he is my inspiration.

Two years later—that's two years without drugs and without sex—I started to date. I did not look for sex dates with people I thought could "open me up." I just tried to meet someone. Have a conversation. See where it went. Because I had learned that forcing myself to be alone, to not trust, to never let someone in was the worst lie of all.

So here I am. Writing again. Sober. Using words. I drink but even that I keep a watchful eye on now.

I try to make the right decisions without the aid of chemicals (I eventually came off the anti-depressants too) or as few chemicals as possible. I don't classify alcohol in this group of chemicals. I drink and enjoy drinking, and have not had to quit that to stop using meth.

At least now as I sit here, with my canvas and my paints and colors, I like to think that if you ask me what was drawn underneath, I might tell you the truth.

No Longer a Disgrace
Jay C.

"Disgrace," my father whispered from his deathbed.

"Excuse me?" I asked

"Disgrace" he repeated.

"Is this how you are going out?" I responded.

"It's how I feel," he said with a shrug.

I had been traveling over ten hours to get to my father's hospital room from my home in New York City. We were in Hanover, New Hampshire, at the Dartmouth Hitchcock Hospital where Dad was being treated for a blood disorder, myelodysplasia, which means the bone marrow stops making blood cells. Although he and my mother are from the Boston area, which is where they raised me, they had a ski house in Vermont. My father wanted to spend his remaining time there. It felt very foreign to me.

Except for childhood winter ski weeks or occasional Saturday ski day trips, I have very little connection to the Vermont or New Hampshire areas. I would have rather had my father in the area where we lived as a family. In this extremely uncomfortable situation, a familiar town would have provided some much needed comfort. This was my first time in Hanover, and the new surroundings made me feel more isolated and alien.

Almost a decade before this hospital visit, my father

disowned me for being gay. Although I hadn't lived in his house since I left for college, I did enjoy my yearly visits with my parents, four sisters, and a myriad of their boyfriends, relatives, and friends who always stopped by the house. During these visits there was always a dynamic of subterranean hurtfulness, just below the surface, but we really did have a good time together. In spite of that, it's still that way with most of my family. We're far from perfect, but I really enjoy spending time with most of my sisters and their families. We have a large extended family with many nieces, nephews, brothers-in-law, cousins, aunts, uncles, and friends. Until my banishment, family events were often a time to put aside differences and celebrate being together. After my father made his decree, most of my family feared his wrath, and went along. Our family entered a very dark time.

I had spent much of my life avoiding having to tell my parents I was gay, or even facing it myself. Because I had four sisters, I was very comfortable around girls and preferred their company. Because I had so many girlfriends, some boys in junior high school despised me. I became the target for a group of guys who teased me unmercifully, calling me "fag" and sometimes beating me up. Some days I would leave school and run home and cry all night, skipping dinner. I learned to perfect my people-pleasing skills and worked harder than anyone, by shoveling neighbor's walkways, cutting their lawns, baby-sitting their kids. If I could have gotten my rage-filled mother to stop screaming, or people to stop calling me "fag," I would have done anything.

In eighth grade, I took a standardized reading and comprehension test. One of the stories in the test focused on the duties of a US Congressional page. I loved the story and decided I wanted to be a page. It became my focus for the next three years. Although my grades were mediocre, I beefed up my resume by running for every student council position, volunteered at every opportunity, and joined any organization that would take me. I was desperate to get away from home and start anew. Finally, in my junior year of high school, I received a call from my congresswoman. I had been accepted into the summer program.

My dream had come true.

Before I left for DC, I had smoked a little pot and gotten drunk only a few times. Within a few weeks of arrival, with a fresh start and new identity, I was introduced to drugs and alcohol. I became a nightly drinker and smoked pot at least three times a day. After the page program, I came home to finish my senior year. I felt as if my life had peaked at fifteen years of age. I was afraid that I had already reached my goal and life was going to be downhill from here. This feeling of my life being already over is a recurring theme that I still wrestle with, even after years of sobriety. It's a feeling that often haunts me, but I have to work hard on not giving in to the feeling, because it's never been true. My life will be over when I die. Not before.

So, to avoid this anxiety, for my senior year of high school, I started getting high as soon as I woke up. I lost all desire in life, except to get high. I almost didn't graduate because I was too stoned and missed too many gym classes. I was always very athletic but the thought of going to the locker room, changing into my gym clothes, and running onto a field 100 yards away seemed as futile as trying to fly by flapping my arms.

Miraculously, I graduated and my overall performance offset my senior year. I got accepted into one of two schools to which I had applied. When I got the good news, I treated myself to a visit to one of my friends from the page program who lived in Texas. We had a blast, staying high or drunk for ten days. The day I came home, I realized I was gay. I don't know if I was in love with my Texas friend, but a voice went off inside me, saying, "You're gay."

I started freaking out. I was screaming inside, "No! No! No!"

I was seventeen years old and I thought that if I was really gay, I had to die before I was twenty-one, because that was when true adulthood set in, and I could not manage being a gay adult. It wasn't what I envisioned for myself. It was not just my family; it was society who forbid it. I had never known a gay man. I'd heard that if you are gay, you will die lonely, broken, alcoholic, and if lucky, murdered at a young age by a straight boy (or boys) you try to seduce.

During college I was a bundle of nerves, my anxiety was through the roof. As a kid I was a bed-wetter and was terrified of anyone finding out. Now I had a secret that was much more potent than that, and if anyone ever found out, I would kill myself. There was no other alternative. I made some great friends in college, some I still love dearly today, but back then, I could never tell them. I pitted girls against each other, telling one I was sleeping with the other, which was why I would not sleep with her. My lies caused everyone great heartache. I would often spend six to eight hours in the library staring at the same page in my textbook, trying to talk myself out of being gay. People thought I studied so hard. Little did they know I wasn't learning a thing. But at this point in life, my only coping tools were to get high and drink. They masked the chronic anxiety and depression.

Around my sophomore year I started to get really paranoid after I smoked pot. I thought people could read my mind and could identify me as gay. So I stopped smoking pot, but my drinking escalated. I loved beer, wine, and tequila. I started to black out, or lose the memory of what I did. When this happened, I loved getting together with my friends, to crack open a beer at 7 a.m. and try to piece together the happenings of the night before. I often drove in this condition. Some nights I saw four lanes instead of two, and I remember thinking, "Please, let me crash into a tree and be done with it."

Miraculously, I graduated from college and headed for Europe, to run away. I landed a job as a ski instructor in the Tyrolean Alps and stayed for almost two years. Since I had to be in good physical condition I started to monitor my beer intake.

When I came back to the US, my father was hoping I would settle down in his insurance company. He was surprised that, two days later, I was on a train headed to New York City. I had no plan; I just knew I needed to be famous. I felt so bad about myself that the only way I felt I could be accepted was to overcompensate and become über-famous.

Instead, I became a New York cliché, an actor and waiter. My drinking became more periodic. I didn't drink every day, because I needed to work on my "instrument." About once every two weeks, I scheduled a night out to get "shit-faced" with my friends at some dive bar.

Finally, in my late twenties, I landed a role in a controversial gay play that ran for almost a year off-Broadway. I thought my "star" had arrived. I had a girlfriend and a boyfriend, each married to different spouses, and I thought I had the world by the balls. *This is why I came to New York City*, I thought.

My girlfriend was a model I met in acting class. One of the things that attracted me to her was her flasks, which always matched her dresses. She had a car and lived off of Park Avenue. She was also a great beard; to the world and myself. She gave me a glimmer of hope that I could be straight.

On the closing night of the play, I took a hit of ecstasy, smoked a joint, and drank a bottle of wine. The next morning I woke up in an apartment on 5th Street between Avenues A and B, not a great neighborhood in 1987. I was naked, and the four other men in bed with me were too. I don't know how I got there, and two of the men, hard-partying friends of my boyfriend, visiting from L.A., had AIDS.

I was shaking. *Oh my God, this is just like college, ten years earlier*, I thought. I looked around and saw the naked L.A. guys. My boyfriend was lying next to me. I woke him, asking, "What happened?"

No sex, he assured me, but he did tell me I was thrown out of the Pyramid Club, a nearly impossible feat since the clientele resembled that in the bar scene of *Star Wars*. He said I hit two people, guys from L.A., and that I bit one of them and drank his blood. He told me that after they threw me out of the club, I was in my underwear banging my head against the sidewalk, yelling, "Nobody loves me!"

My first thought was, "I'm a vampire." I did not think, "I am an alcoholic," although on some level I knew I was.

The death wish I held in my teenage years was quickly becoming a reality. All I needed was one more night in a black out in New York City, and I could contract AIDS—or worse.

For about two weeks I felt that the gig was up, that it was time to sober up, but I didn't know what to do. Alcohol was clearly not working for me anymore. I had gone to a meeting in a college with a priest. I was doing a paper on alcoholism at our school, and so, I was doing "research." I knew that someday I would be back. I just wish it didn't take me ten years, but I wasn't ready then.

Finally, I called A.A. That was August 8, 1987, and I haven't had a drink or drug since. My obsession to drink has never been lifted, but neither has my desire to stay sober. I want my sobriety more than anything and I love being sober, even during the dark times, of which there have been many.

I got sober when I was twenty-eight. After a few years of hearing about rigorous honesty, I felt it was time to be honest with my parents. I was openly gay in New York City and to many of my family and friends who lived elsewhere. I had just never told my parents. My father was a devout Catholic, and he was recovering from a colon cancer diagnosis. I hid behind the words, "If I told him who I really am, I would kill him."

But our relationship was deteriorating, and I had nothing to lose. The proverbial straw that broke the camel's back was the summer of 1991. I was passing through Boston to visit some high school friends and made plans to see my parents for dinner. It was over ninety degrees, and I wore shorts. I figured we would go to his country club where they have a terrace and people eat burgers and sandwiches in their tennis shorts. We had done this for decades. On this evening, things were different. He was furious. He canceled the reservation and yelled, "Men don't wear shorts; they get married and wear pants." I was humiliated, and I left for New York and stewed in my resentful juices for two months.

Finally, I called my parents and told them I was coming home, and arranged a time when they should both be there. When I arrived at their house, my father started right in, talking about the shorts. I said it wasn't the shorts that bothered him, and he knew it. He looked at me stricken. When I mentioned the word *gay*, he howled, leaped from his chair, crashed into the wall, and screamed at my mother, "Did you hear what he said, he takes it up the ass!"

He then called me "an abomination," and said things like, "You are not my son," "Thank God your grandfather is not alive to see this," and "I never want to see you again."

Within a couple of minutes, he grabbed his car keys off the counter and was gone, yelling at me to be out of his house by the time he got back. My mother, who is usually the screamer of the family, kept curiously quiet. She fed me a bowl of the corn chowder she had prepared for my visit, and I left.

But my father kept his word. He took down all the pictures of me around the house and forbade anyone to speak about me. For a decade I missed family holidays, christenings, weddings, and the reason I was given was always the same: "I have to choose between you and Dad, but Dad is dying, and this could be his last Christmas," or Thanksgiving, wedding, fill in the occasion.

When I got sober in 1987, I mostly worked in the theater. New York City, especially in the theater world, was on the front lines of the AIDS/HIV epidemic. I remember when my father disowned me and my friends were dying I had moments of doubt. "What if the Christian fundamentalists are right and AIDS is a curse from God for being gay? Our families, society, government, everyone hates us, and God is killing us with this horrible disease." Fortunately, I had learned in the program that just because we have doubt or irrational thoughts, it doesn't make them true. I also knew drinking would never make it better.

The second toughest time in my life so far, other than high school, was my first seven years of sobriety. I really came to terms with being gay. I stopped trying to cover with "girlfriends," and my career was non-existent, and I didn't know what I wanted to do. I was so passionate about acting and a life in theater, and when I got sober, the passion faded. But I stayed in it for another decade because it was my identity and I didn't have the tools to make a change. Besides, it was in the middle of the AIDS crisis and my young talented friends were dying all around me.

I just clung to life, day to day, not drinking, going to meetings, and quietly freaking out. To top it off, my parent's rejection added more pain, and I felt I had very little support in the world. I was too ashamed to tell people about my family's treatment of me—that would prove that I was unlovable and somehow validate that I was the failure my parents seemed to think.

Fortunately I got a good therapist, and after a few years I began writing and picked up a camera to document what was going on in the gay community in the late '80s. I followed a close friend for the last year and half of his life as he died of AIDS. I had no filmmaking experience but I applied the tools of the program. Just shoot one scene, today. The next day, do the same. I knew if I didn't drink I would figure it out. And that has become my motto.

That film helped me find my voice and I have been developing it ever since. I have gone on to make more films, and with the new technologies for the Internet and mobile platforms, I continue to create video content.

So back to New Hampshire, and my father's hospital room. It's now 2001, and I am thirteen years sober. I never walk around in public holding my Big Book, but on this day I did. I clutched it like a missionary using a crucifix to ward off an evil vampire. I sat in my father's room, just the two of us. I was so enraged, I wanted to take the pillow from under his head and smother him. Who would have blamed me?

Since I wasn't going to commit patricide, Plan B was to yell, "Fuck you, die you bastard!" Then storm out of the hospital and never see him again.

I knew that however I reacted I would have to live with that choice for the rest of my life. I felt that my thirteen years of recovery—not drinking, regularly going to meetings, service, practicing the Twelve Steps and the Twelve Traditions to the best of my ability, and weekly psychotherapy appointments, all this work had prepared me for this moment. Besides, I had heard about sober-death-bed reconciliations between estranged parents and children, and I had mine coming.

Before I opened the Big Book I thought to myself, *OK, God, whatever, wherever you are, the page I open to is how I should handle this situation, because I am really confused.*

I cracked open the Book to "How It Works," pages 66-67. It reads, "We realized that the people who wronged us were perhaps spiritually sick. Though we did not like their symptoms and the way they disturbed us, they, like ourselves, were sick too. We asked God to help us show them the same tolerance, pity, and patience that we would cheerfully grant a sick friend. When a person offended us, we said to ourselves, 'This is a sick man. How can I be helpful to him? God save me from being angry. Thy will be done.'"

I actually felt relief after reading this random passage. As much as I fantasized about creating a scene and storming out of the hospital, I also wanted to see this through. So, I did what I always do whenever I find myself in a situation where I need to take an action and I am not sure about the next step. I went back to my beginner tools and asked myself, "Does it need to be said by me? Does it need to be said now? Does it need to be said by me now?"

Whenever I ran through those three questions, the answer, 98% of the time, was "no."

I also ran through, HALT: Am I Hungry, Angry, Lonely or Tired? If I met any of these criteria, I held off on responding verbally or taking an action until I was rested, fed, and have talked with people I trust. Those three things took the edge off my anger, too. These sayings are cliché, and I cringe when I hear them repeated in meetings, but they work.

At that moment in my father's hospital room, I was filled with rage, despair, exhaustion and confusion, and I felt that no one understood me. Everyone was focused on my father's dying, asking me, "Isn't it horrible, he's dying?" and "Aren't you sad?" But I wasn't. I was enraged that he chose to disown me, his only son, for being who I am, and that, even on his death bed, he still stood by his decision.

I tried explaining it to my sisters and other family members and friends, but they were lost in their own grief and didn't want to hear anything but loving thoughts for my father.

So, even though I was not hungry, I went to the cafeteria and ate a sandwich and immediately feel better. Then, I had the strength to handle what was coming my way. It's one of the gifts of sobriety. Sometimes, when I don't know what to do, I do nothing. Or I do something so banal like take a walk and eat a sandwich, and suddenly I am transformed.

I returned to my father's hospital room, and my sister was feeding him. Not knowing about our conversation, that he had just called me a "disgrace," my sister was all smiles. "Jay, do you want to feed Dad?" she asked innocently.

My first reaction was, "Are you nuts?!"

But then I remembered those lines: "This is a sick man. How can I be helpful to him? God save me from being angry." I looked at my father, he shrugged, meaning, it was OK with him. I picked up the spoon and instead of jamming it down his throat, I didn't say anything, and I fed him. When he was done, I cleaned him up and left.

Less than two months later, on September 11, 2001, the World Trade Center was attacked by Al-Qaeda and Osama Bin Laden. My partner and I lived less than a mile from the Trade Center. That morning we took our usual run down West Broadway, marveling at the beauty of the day and magnificence of the towers. We were so elated to be in New York City: "Is there any place more vibrant and beautiful?"

A few hours later, the planes hit, and our world was forever changed. My partner was downtown and he saw the tower after the first plane crashed. He was traumatized by it for months afterward.

Two days after that, I get another call from home. "He's dying. You need to come now," my sister said, "Don't you know what is going on down here?" I said.

The smell of burnt rubber and steel permeated our apartment, furniture, and clothes. Our neighborhood was on lock down, and we had to pass checkpoints every ten blocks. My partner, traumatized from the seeing the buildings on fire, begged me not to go, but I promised to be back in three days.

Once back in Vermont, I thought, *What am I doing here?*

My real family, my partner, was in New York City, and he needed me. My father was in the other room, lying in a diaper, and wouldn't speak to me, and my mother was drunk and calling me an ingrate.

I went to join my father. He was in his bedroom lying on a hospital bed. The diaper he wore was not to collect urine or feces, but blood. Blood oozed from his penis. He was bleeding to death. The two of us, who had barely seen or spoken to one another in more than ten years, were lying next to each other in beds about twelve inches apart. I was in my underwear because the weekend was extraordinarily hot, and my parents' Vermont mountain house didn't have air conditioning. The TV was always on, reporting news coverage from Ground Zero, and I wished to be home with my partner.

Every three hours my father let out a groan. I got up and helped him to the bathroom. I pulled down his diaper, which was brimming with blood, and dropped it on the floor. Blood splatters hit the floor and lower walls. I cleaned him up, put a new diaper on him, and brought him back to bed. I went back to the bathroom and cleaned the blood off the white tiles. I did this because of that one line in the Big Book:"This is a sick man. How can I be helpful to him? God save me from being angry." He was going out, I was staying. I was sober, and this was what I had learned in sobriety. My father and I didn't speak for the entire weekend. When I left I told him I loved him. He said, "Thank you."

Those were our last words to one another.

Three weeks later he died. My sisters, my mother, aunt, and I were at his bedside. I was relieved because I now had my family back, yet so sad that my father and I had not had our tearful deathbed reconciliation. The one I always had heard happens to people when they get sober. I was sober, but it hadn't happen the way I'd heard it in the "rooms," and I was pissed.

I always thought if I stayed sober throughout this situation I would be rewarded by my father saying,"I'm sorry, I love you and you will always be my son." I guess allowing me to change his bloody diapers and his thank you were his way of saying, "I love you," but his breathless, "Disgrace," still leaves me in disbelief.

One of the most important lessons I have learned in sobriety is that things sometimes do not work out the way I want. I thought that since I didn't drink and was committed to recovery, I deserved good things to happen to me. Even though I knew the "good thing" or "gift" is being sober, I expected more. It wasn't until I was sober for almost a couple of decades that I realized being sober is a gift because it gives me choices. It empowers me to find ways to accept the situation or change my thoughts and behaviors responsibly.

It is never easy, and in my twenty-fifth year of continuous sobriety, I still need a lot of help. About a year after my father's death, I found myself in a rage all the time. I was angry and scared and dealing with post-9/11 trauma. I couldn't accept my father's death and still wished for his proclamation of love and devotion. Then the economy took a nosedive.

I kept going to meetings and shared how miserable I was. People told me to "keep coming back," but I felt worse and disconnected. Nothing worked and nothing changed. I felt that if someone told me one more time "to get on my knees and read page 449 of the Big Book," I would go ballistic. I was tired of hearing myself sound like a broken record at meetings, so I stopped sharing.

But I never stopped going to meetings. I had enough experience to know that meetings usually improve my mood. Besides, I am always spooked when I hear people say they stopped going to meetings and relapsed. As much as I want to drink, I want my sobriety more.

About this time a friend from a twelve-step fellowship told me about a five-day codependency program at the Caron Foundation in Pennsylvania. Feeling pretty desperate and in need of the extra help, I signed myself in. I thought to myself on the bus ride to Pennsylvania, *I am in my fifteenth year of sobriety and I am just not getting it. I am failing at sobriety. Maybe I am one of those constitutionally incapable ones, and just can't be "happy, joyous and free."*

Even though I hadn't had a drink, I still thought about it and wanted relief. I felt trapped in my life and miserable. When I checked in at the Caron Foundation, I thought I had made a really big and expensive mistake. *This is really dumb*, I thought. *I already know what I need to do: don't drink and go to meetings, help another alcoholic, so I should just go home.* But I felt scared enough to stay.

The Caron Foundation reminded me how lovable I am and taught me that although my parents' rage did some serious damage, it had nothing to do with me. What a waste, these inauthentic images of ourselves that we carry through life. But how fortunate we are that if we don't drink, we get a chance to change ourselves for the better.

I love being sober, even on my darkest days, because I know the darkness will pass and lightness will come again. For years, even in sobriety, I was chronically dissatisfied, no matter what my achievements. I diminished everything. I am my mother's son that way. But after many years in sobriety, I am discovering a better way of handling my thoughts. After a bad day at work, instead of licking my wounds and thinking things like, *My life is over and I need to quit my job, but I will never find a new one, I am totally fucked*, I can think to myself, *It's not that bad. You know it. You're just tired. Don't quit today. If you are still miserable in a few weeks, OK, then begin an official job-search, but don't do anything rash.* I have learned to talk myself down from "the ledge." Besides, life is passing, and I don't want to waste it by being as inconsolable as I have been.

Fortunately, the lighter days outnumber the dark, which is why I never stop going to meetings. Meetings aren't, as many people make them out to be, everything I need but they, and the Twelve Steps and the Twelve Traditions are a great foundation.

At the suggestion of another friend in A.A., I started attending Al-Anon meetings. I was told it would help with my "anger." I still don't understand how Al-Anon works, it's not as tangible as putting down the drink, but I go and get a great deal of benefit from it. The program helps me set boundaries for myself and encourages me to focus on my assets instead of always focusing on my character defects. It also helps me be clearer and more consistent in my relationships. It's an extremely gentle program, and I usually fold in one to two meetings a week in addition to at least two A.A. meetings a week. I still go to therapy, exercise regularly, and practice meditation and yoga. I am terrible at meditation and yoga, but especially love the practice of yoga. I take at least one class a week, and when I do it, it feels right. It helps me slow down, which is something I want. I am tired of drama and war zones. I want more peace.

Finally, my partner of sixteen years and I bought a weekend house in upstate New York, a couple of hours outside the city. It's a sweet house that overlooks the Berkshire Mountains. Every day, whether the sun comes up over the mountain or not, light bathes our bedroom and the mountains are the first thing we see. I have never woken up in a more beautiful place and have never felt so comforted and grateful. Each morning I wake up there, my first thought of the day is, *This is all because I am sober, thank you.*

I have what I need and want for nothing, and I have never been more grateful. I have never felt more engaged and motivated to be alive, and it is all because I choose not to drink one day at a time. And for the first time in my life, I can admit, if I drank, I would have too far to fall. For this inconsolable alcoholic, that is a miracle.

Things I Know Better Now
Leslie L. Smith

The first thing a gay man ever gave me was a can of Schaffer's beer. It was not my first drink of alcohol, but it may be the most remarkable drink of my life. The man who gave me the beer, whom we'll call John (even though he called everyone else Mary), was the first out gay man I had ever met, and he gave me the beer, and many subsequent others, on the first day I knew him.

It was the summer I had turned fifteen, and I had joined the cast of a summer-stock play at the local college in my hometown. John was having a "get-to-know-you" party for the cast on the first night of rehearsal. He invited me during the rehearsal, and I rode with him to his house after. The first thing he did was to get me a beer from the fridge to enjoy while he changed. He told me that night I was free to help myself to whatever booze was in the house. He knew I was gay. I knew I was gay, but I had never felt what it was to be recognized this way. For me, this unspoken understanding was a new kind of electricity that had buzzed around the air, nameless, all day. It was almost empowering, but I was too young to know how to harness that. The world around us wanted neither of us to be the way we were. Yet John was out, and more than that, he was open and friendly. He was more than OK with himself, he seemed proud of who he was.

Part of me wanted to come out to John that night, but I could not say the words we both knew to be true. John and his other gay male friends were fawning over me most of the night, in a way that made me very uncomfortable, but I also did not want the attention to stop, so I managed my feelings by drinking. John kept intimating that we shared something, and I got the idea he wanted me to admit that I was gay like him. This went on the entire night, and all the while he, and all his gay friends, kept encouraging me to drink up.

The message was clear. Alcohol was meant as lubricant. The gay men at this party were telling me that booze would help me be different. And I *needed* the help. It was hard to admit I shared this identity with John and his friends, as I felt I was nothing like them. I never could fully accept them, even if I knew we were the same. They loved to do drag and watch Bette Davis movies. While I liked Bette Davis movies, I hated the idea of dressing as a woman, at that age it seemed to me like becoming what we were hated for—like giving straight haters what they wanted. I was also an athlete (on the swim team) and liked to be outdoors, but John and his friends didn't like me hanging out with the jocks I swam with. They lusted after hairless twinks in fragrance ads, and I wanted the big, burly men of the World Wrestling Federation. I had found my people but I still felt alone.

My parents were both conservative and country. Most of my extended family is the kind of southern Christian that remains convinced that a reason beyond their understanding must explain why science contradicts the Bible, and biblical version of things should be taken literally. Much of my life, my well-educated mother deferred to my less-educated father's idea of parenting— as this was her duty as a Christian wife. As a child, Dad passed for suburban middle-class, but even then, he leaned toward a backwoods kind of mentality. I was taught to swim by being thrown off a boat into deep water. I was taught to hunt and fish and made to kill things, even when it clearly traumatized me. My squeamishness and my intellectual nature were things my parents could not quite ever accept, as they were the stock of country folk—living off the land was what was required to survive, so a certain hardness was required as well. I lacked this hardness, but worse, I had no wish to acquire it.

Growing up, the most common question either of my parents asked me was, "What's wrong with you?" usually in an angry tone that convinced me that I was some sort of freakish embarrassment.

I took these messages to heart and became convinced I was broken. *"What's wrong with me?"* would become *the* question of my life, rearing its ugly, judgmental cry in my head each time I felt that I was outside of any group, made any mistake, fell down, or whenever I wanted something I couldn't have. As a child, an answer to this question would whisper in my head, "I like boys."

Between ages nine and twelve I tried to force myself to fit my parents' expectations and often felt suicidal. I had no friends. I took solace in comics and literature. By the time I was fifteen and met John, TV's *Dynasty* had begun to teach me about gay men—and that not all the world believed as my parents and their community did. I got past my suicidal thoughts, and began to believe that if I could just get out of that small town, the question would just disappear. If I could get out I would travel, see the world, stay free, and experience as much as I could. And from age twelve to the day I left, I hungered for that journey to begin.

But during those years I also began searching for something more tangible that resembled what I felt, but finding real-life examples of gay men to model myself after was difficult. By the time I was a teen, I was bold enough to make subtle passes at strange men whom I caught watching me. Sometimes I got lucky, other times I got into dangerous and sometimes violent situations. Each of those violent scenes reinforced the idea that there was something wrong with me that needed to be fixed. Another result of my sexual boldness was that I began to find local men who were "like" me. They were mostly married and closeted, lying and unhappy. The idea of telling the number of lies required to actually marry a woman seemed much more immoral than simply being gay. To hurt someone else that much seemed cruel. But people, gay and straight alike, acted like the other choice was more acceptable.

From a very young age, all this strife seemed to me to be the result of religion. Faith and belief seemed to me to lead to a sad end. They were both blind and limiting. They were concepts riddled with fear-based traps. Those traps seemed designed to keep people in their place, to keep them from amassing experience and from becoming more plentiful and productive than what they could make from their own yards—coveting such things was sinful. And that, to me, seemed ridiculously lame.

So when I got that first can of beer, and found a group of men and women who didn't lie, who simply were who they were, I was more than happy to join their ritual drinking —to be merry and gather the Dutch courage required to face such an unfair world.

Finally, at seventeen, I did come out, at least to John and his group of friends, and they wanted to celebrate by drinking and putting on wigs. I accepted the drinks and declined the wig. But they all wore them, dresses, and makeup to indoctrinate me into the gay world. I didn't like it. I felt John and his friends judged me for not conforming to their ways. After my coming-out party, I felt more alone than ever. Even at my coming-out party the question of my life would resound in my head, *"What is wrong with me?"*

The only thing I had to bond me to that group was drinking. I accepted that as enough; perhaps I thought it was as close to being accepted as I might ever come. In my first few years of being out, before being out and sober, the gay men I would meet would give me lots of booze, drugs, and even several STDs, all before I was of legal drinking age. These things were given to me, a minor, disguised as a tool of empowerment. At the time, I believed they all represented steps toward freedom and self-actualization. Using alcohol and drugs was an active expression of my ability to choose a different life path than the one my parents were planning for me. I believed alcohol and drugs gave me the power to be exactly who I was—even in a world that wanted nothing more than for me to get AIDS and die, as this was the truth of being young and gay in Arkansas during the '80s.

Every gay event I attended as a teen was built with the intent of drinking and using—to oblivion. They were not social events for discussing art or culture, and having a glass of wine. They were backwoods affairs in dry counties complete with kegs, whiskey shooters, and Everclear punch, all of which were provided with the sole purpose of getting everyone bombed out of their skull. That is how I learned to drink. And that is how I drank, as frequently as possible, until the day I stopped at age twenty.

When I participated in these affairs, it was more than simply needing to belong. It was an active act of rebellion against the values the church-based community was trying to force me to accept. Values that were, in turn, trying to suppress who I was. But I was hardly self-aware enough to know that then. I was simply acting out, hurting myself with the tremendous amount of anger I felt.

When I left for college in Dallas, Texas, I no longer had familial structures to rely on. I was in a city (not the country) and that came with plenty of shiny new distractions. It was big change from my Arkansas small town. Gay bars were but a short cab ride from campus. In my first week I discovered JR's Bar and Grill. I thought I had died and gone to heaven. Beautiful butch men were everywhere, and they were all offering me sex and free booze. I threw myself into the bars, forsaking classes and my studies. For what felt like the first time in my life, I had found men who looked like what I wanted to be— masculine, confident, and comfortable with themselves— and they were not on campus, but in the bar.

My small-town high school had ill-prepared me for a world-class college. I was behind before I ever arrived. It would take me a semester to figure that out. Once I did, I felt ashamed that my choice to carouse with the new men in my life had cost me my GPA. To drown the shame, I drank some more, and then I lost my scholarship. So I drank some more, and I lost all my financial aid, until finally I was forced to withdraw from school before being expelled. Now out of the dorm, I had no place to live, and so I started crashing with different friends from the bar and tricking for overnight stays as much as I could. Shortly after leaving school, I was arrested for "public intoxication." A friend bailed me out and dropped me at the home of a man I had been seeing. That day they both suggested I would be happier if I tried drinking less.

By the time I was twenty, I was beginning to shake the idea that "gay" was what was "wrong" with me. But on some level, if gay was the wrong answer, the question still seemed valid. It had a tight hold on my concept of self. The question was not going to leave just because I accepted that I was gay as a part of a natural order.

Instead, it needed a new answer. These two men had just offered it to me.

My mother had long warned me that A.A. might be in my future, since her father and his father had both died in alcohol-related "incidents." I had also witnessed my father's father drink himself to death instead of seeking treatment for a ruptured appendix. Now a man I was seeing was suggesting I drank too much. I didn't try drinking less, I went to A.A. Within a few nights, I sat in a gay meeting and said, "I think I might be an alcoholic." To which a gold lamé-clad drag queen answered, "Oh honey, if you're here, then there is no doubt."

I heeded my mother's warnings. I quickly affirmed I was an alcoholic, and admitted that was what was wrong with me. The Program and its members promised me that I could recover from my "spiritual malady." This concept quickly became the new answer to the question of my life. *"What was wrong with me?"* A spiritual malady.

This began a time when being a gay alcoholic was the center of my identity. The Program and the activities associated with it defined my social circles, my personal relationships, and even, to an extent, my professional development. The Program's "spirituality" did not seem to impose morality and restriction, but instead it offered a structure within which I might find my own morals. It also promised a "new freedom and a new happiness," words I thought seemed sweeter than the promise of heaven, because at such a tender age of twenty, I was unsure I had ever known either.

I was about thirty days sober when I went to court. The judge offered to expunge my record because of my age, and to forgo probation because I had taken myself to A.A. He said, "I'm proud of you, son, stick with it and you'll go far." I left court and cried. The path to A.A. seemed almost fated. And that was enough to make the concept of God work for a while. I felt I was supposed to find my way to the rooms, I was supposed to avoid the fate of my grandparents. I was clearly genetically predetermined to be an addict and that was *"what was wrong with me."* Life leading me to A.A. just might be Divine intervention.

I returned to meetings and I did what the people in A.A. told me to do: I found the people who had what I wanted, and I did as they did. That was easy. A.A. was full of men who had what I wanted, but that's because they were grown and I was not. As a drunken twenty-year old, what I wanted was a place of my own and a sense of purpose. As my mind and heart grew sober, my twelve-step work revealed that, in spite of avoiding my parents' traps, I had much fear in me. And by getting to know those fears, I also got to know my hopes and dreams, and I moved to New York City to chase them.

Once there, A.A.'s promises quickly came true— beyond my wildest dreams. As cliché as it sounds, it will always be true. But what is also a fact is that dreams can come true, but life doesn't stop where that happens, it keeps moving, and on multiple tracks. My career could be great but a close friend could be dying. I could meet a great guy and be broke and out of work. I couldn't figure out why I couldn't make it all work at once.

In New York, I quickly came into my own and had a remarkable first decade in sobriety, despite the fact that that decade was marred by the loss of many friends and would-be lovers. It was almost a daily ritual to go to a meeting and then go to the hospital to sit with a friend who was dying of AIDS. Weekends were memorial services, dancing, and my part-time job at the gym. In those days, I had as much A.A. fellowship in St. Vincent's Hospital rooms and cafeteria as I did in any coffee shop. But by the mid-'90s men had stopped dying as they had done before. Then my mother got sick. I went home to Arkansas for eight weeks to care for her.

Her sudden fatal condition, resulting from a reaction to chemo for a non-aggressive cancer, gave me the chance to put what I learned in A.A.'s fellowship, and in the halls and rooms of St Vincent's, to work in caring for her, my father, and my sister. During that six-week period, as she died slowly, when my family seemed so uncertain, I could be strong and steady. I could talk to the doctors and challenge them without fear of what they had to say. Me, assertive and in control of a stressful situation— that was something my family had never seen. When Mom died, I demanded the funeral home deal with her in specific ways she would have wanted, and my father cried and thanked me. I felt proud of providing for them. In spite of all this, the day after my mother was buried, my father seemed happy that he could finally ask me to leave. The question of my life, *"What's wrong with me?"* immediately restarted its seemingly endless loop.

Each time there were bumps, stumbles, or falls in my life, the question resurfaced. But in those days it always came with the answer, "You're an alcoholic, get to a meeting." I followed those instructions and A.A. took the place of my family; it nurtured me and taught me right from wrong in terms I could live with.

For the first decade of sobriety, almost everything A.A. taught me brought me comfort and strength. But by the time I was approaching my tenth anniversary, I was starting to feel detached from the rooms. My sponsor told me that with each decade of sobriety, you either get a new God, a new program, or you get drunk. I was afraid of getting drunk, so I tried to make God "bigger."

Early in sobriety, God had been a random force that moved me forward to the amazing places I found myself. Mostly, God was a shorter word for "coincidences," which my life seemed full of. But over time as I stayed sober, that seemed insufficient. By my eleventh and twelfth year, in the aftermath of 9/11, it was even more lacking. And as "He" seemed lacking, I was being told the work ahead of me was to make him bigger. But I couldn't really think of how to do that. The more I tried to revise "Him," the less real "He" seemed. I tried a few new Gods on for size, including "Science of the Mind" existential churches, and those didn't work. God became a draft of a bad novel rewritten so many times the kernel of what had worked was long lost. I also tried, as my sponsor had suggested, a few new twelve-step programs, but none of them fit either. I was at a loss for where to go, but I didn't get drunk. Instead, I kept going to meetings and I grew more steadily unhappy.

I heard that recurring question, *"What's wrong with me?"* begin to grow louder, and my answer to it began to soften. I would return to the rooms, looking for a fix. But without a Higher Power, A.A.'s sayings and practices were somehow incomplete. They all insisted I believe in something, and I couldn't find anything that worked. I felt like a fake. I felt as though I was beginning to fall down, in spite of the fact that the structures supporting me seemed as solid as they had ever been. I was no longer sure that what I wanted could be found in A.A. But I continued to go, in part out of fear of using (or rather of what might happen to me if I did), and in part out of habit, because the foundations of my life were built on the teachings of A.A. and hearing them aloud in a room was affirming, if not always comforting.

I felt lost, and I tried to hide that I no longer believed, mostly from myself. I could not actively tell people that the steps, which asked everyone to find God, were the right answer—I could only say they were *an* answer (which is in line with what A.A. says, that these steps are "suggested"). But I knew them well enough to fake it, and

I seemed expected to play this role by my fellow A.A. members, so I did. This left me crushed with the guilt of being a liar, or a phony. Finally, I had to admit to myself that I had never really believed in God, I had only tried to believe—and I had tried really hard—and I had failed. I was without a Higher Power and A.A.'s rhetoric, which I had adopted as my own, told me that left to my own devices, I would, most surely, end up drunk in a gutter somewhere, or worse. What was left? Nothing. The day I realized this—let's just say it was a very scary place to be.

During this second decade I had also achieved a lot. I held a lead management role in two of the largest disaster responses in history, got a B.A, and then managed to start a Ph.D. program that accepted me without a Masters. As A.A. suggested, I credited all my successes to God (in spite of the fact that I could no longer conceive of Him) and the Program. But the more I accomplished and the more I excelled, the emptier I felt—and the more I felt I had to prove myself. I quit working out for the first time in my life, and I grew fat. I told myself I was way too busy and important for something as trivial as the gym. But I still managed to squeeze in meetings, an average of one every two weeks.

There, speakers with just three to four years of sobriety talked with certainty about their lives, a certainty that I knew would be undone by the trails of what waited ahead for anyone in recovery. At first I thought it was almost quaint to see the post-newcomers at work and to feel so wise and mature, but year after year it all got old. And I began to feel lonely. Soon, I sat quietly at the back of every meeting, angry that I had to be there, angry that I owed what I had to the room I now felt trapped in.

In contrast, I found school was not only easy, but fun and life-affirming. But there was little room for God or religion in the halls of NYU. In school, I felt perfectly at home and comfortable with shedding the idea that I needed God. The fact that it was so easy to let Him go was a secret I kept to myself when I went back to A.A. There, I no longer spoke of God, and when others sought my counsel, I usually tried to reflect their own beliefs, rather than express my own.

I continued to go, here and there, just enough, I told myself. I did this because A.A. was my medicine. I was afraid of what would happen if I ever used again. I did this because I was approaching two decades sober and I was young. I did this because I was supposed to be a role model. I was supposed to have wisdom and strength, not anger, questions, and doubt. I hoped that if I kept showing up that I would lose those things. Plus, the Twelfth Step was to carry the message. I continued to show up because it was my duty, since A.A. had saved my life. But more and more, I found I was incapable of espousing its message (without realizing that simply showing up can often be enough).

I looked around the rooms for guidance, for someone who "had what I wanted." I could hardly find anyone in A.A. who had what I'd lost, and so desperately wanted back: confidence. I wanted to once again find my ability to be competent in anything I put my mind to—and to respond effectively to any challenge placed in front of me. But I no longer felt I had the heart for that.

The harder I looked for answers among them, and the less the people in the rooms looked like me, the more they reminded me of my parents seeking comforts of the religious fellowships I had so shunned growing up. They also sounded like my parents, pushing me to believe as they did. Yet, these were my closest friends, my confidants. They were the people who had propped me up when things were bleakest for nearly twenty years. How could all that now feel so different than it had then?

In my twentieth year in A.A., I was laid off from my job and I moved to Florida. After about a year there, I saw a "sober countdown." This is where all the people in the room stand and the group leaders start counting from one. If you have less than a year of continuous sobriety, you sit when they count "one." If you have less than two years, you sit at "two," and so on. As the numbers of years go up, the numbers of people go down. At these countdowns, it is always intimated that the reason for these reducing numbers is that alcoholism has claimed A.A.'s missing brethren. They have succumbed to the disease of alcoholism and are either dead or drunk and unhappy.

I had seen this ritual a hundred or more times over the years, but his time, for the first time, I was struck with a different thought. "They aren't all dead, are they? What about the people who get tired and just choose to leave? Those who find a different way? Where are their numbers?"

For the first time I felt it was an oppressive exercise. I was also among the last to sit. The few men who had more time than I did were at least twenty years my senior, and neither of them had twenty more years sober time than me. If I stayed where I was, in twenty years I would be standing alone as the countdown progressed for almost a decade to get to me. I would once again be standing alone. And that scared me more than using did. What I wanted was to be in the world. I wanted to find the hunger I had as a teen to experience and live in as much of the world as possible, not just the community that was closest to me. And I realized in that moment, that such a hunger was not to be found in the rooms. I needed something other than another twenty years of church basements and the same old drinking stories, despite the fact that those basements and stories had made me who I was.

Shortly after that sobriety countdown came the day

that marked being sober half my life. That day I was not grateful to be sober as I had been for so long. I felt trapped in the rooms and I wanted to be truly free, if just for a while, before all of my life had passed me by. After all, wasn't knowing "a new freedom and a new happiness" a promise of the Program? I had felt that, long ago, but despite my dedication to the rooms, I hadn't felt those things in a long, long time. Was I only supposed to feel it once? Was that supposed to sustain me for fifty years or more?

Suddenly, I had questions that I had never had before. By getting sober so young, had I missed my only chance to thrive with my peers? Had I really felt safe in the rooms because I could be with older, smarter people? Had I missed my legitimate right to experience carefree fun in my life? What might it be like to drop ecstasy at a circuit party? I began to fear I could never know what might have been.

My friends and advisors suggested, as I knew they would, that this was the disease talking, that I was headed for a slip that would claim my life. And I listened to them, as that's what I had been taught to do. But no matter what I did, I couldn't find a center; I couldn't get up again and re-engage with life. The question grew louder than ever, "WHAT'S WRONG WITH ME?"

But now the question had no answer at all. Weeks and weeks went by with this deafening question echoing in my head, repeatedly, with no answer.

Then it finally it happened. I was traveling in London, and I used chemical inhalants in a sexual situation. I did it carelessly. To be fair, I put myself in a dangerous sexual situation where I had a good idea they would be used. It was an act of rebellion—just as it had been when I was young. I needed something, anything, to stop the sound of the question. I was high for the first time in almost twenty-two years and it felt great. I was seventeen again, angry, ready to escape the unfair world, even if it meant hurting myself by acting out. As the sex scene played out, in the back of my mind I thought that when it was over, I would head out to a bar and drown myself in booze, or start looking for new and better ways to take myself higher. But instead, I came so hard that I floated home and went to sleep.

The next day, when it dawned on me I would no longer be able to say I was continuously sober for half my life, I panicked. I avoided the rooms for a few days, and then I went to a meeting and said nothing about what had happened.

As strange as this sounds, when I realized I had used and didn't die or go immediately hurtling down a suicidal path, I didn't understand what was happening. My disease, as A.A. had told me, was supposed to be back in full gear, bigger and stronger than ever. This was supposed to be the end of my world, but instead everything looked and felt pretty normal. Still, I was not overtaken with the urge to kill myself, or use into oblivion. Surprisingly, I did not even want to try a drink. All I wanted was to have twenty-two years of continuous sobriety on the horizon again, but that was gone. I was an A.A. newcomer, and I was at a loss for what to do. So, I tried to pretend it didn't happen. I lied. I made it out as though I had been forced, which was partially true but also partially not. People tried to comfort me, but lying had made it all seem even worse.

The most confusing part of all was, like most people in A.A., I had spent years planning the fantasy slip. I had long lists of what I would do and try if the world ever afforded me the path of using again. The door was now open and I did not even want to walk through it. But I also didn't want to go back to the day before, feeling alone and miserable in the rooms of A.A. I didn't know what to do. I had no idea how to *not* be a gay alcoholic, sober since age twenty. It was all I knew. Eventually, the guilt of my secret would lead me to use again. And the guilt of that led me back to the rooms where I came clean.

Each day I felt I had to go to a meeting and count my days because that's the only way I knew to retrieve what I had lost. But every time I had to count days in an A.A. meeting, it made me feel as though I had fallen; it highlighted my wrongness in a profound, angry, and destructive way. And I used again.

I went back into therapy, and my therapist insisted that A.A. was the only hope I had if I wanted to get sober again. So in spite of not wanting it, I tried. Because, again, it was all I knew and all I was offered.

I was not expecting that as I tried the program again I would rebel against it, much the way as a young child I rebelled against my parent's belief systems. Now that I had used, every unspoken thought and idea I had had about the program's short-comings would get in the way of my ability to get sober again.

During this time, I would come to understand that I knew many gay men in the program who were doing the kind of drugs that I had used, but since they were not drinking, they did not restart their sobriety date. Perhaps I was naive, but I had never imagined this to be true of people in the program. My sober circles had always believed in total abstinence as the only measure of sobriety. While I did not want to return to that kind of rigidity, which no longer fit with the complex world I had come to know, I felt like a hypocrite trying to be in the program and not completely abstinent.

This was when I began to realize that I knew the program backward and forward. People would try to show me the way, and I would take them to the passage in the Big Book that they were misquoting. Every time I tried to be a "newcomer," the shoes didn't fit because my feet were too big—swollen with the knowledge the role of "newcomer" was meant to teach me. I knew that my feet could not get smaller, so somewhere, I thought, there must be bigger shoes.

I started to speak of this in the rooms, to try to find a new way to start over in A.A. When I did I was gently lectured and told to accept a more humble path. The most common message was that if I had used, I had missed something, and I needed to listen, to go back to the beginning and get it right this time. I was repeatedly pushed, or cajoled, back into the role of "newcomer" by almost everyone I knew and everyone I met. A few men who had slipped after long term sobriety showed up with more sympathetic ears, but in the end their advice was the same.

The frustration of trying to make twenty years of old hat seem new and fresh would lead me to use again. And this was seen as proof that I needed to be a newcomer. This began a cycle that lasted about six month, in which I would begin to try many of the chemicals gay men often associate with sex. But I didn't drink. That confused me even more. My therapist said I had "traded addictions." In reality, I did not want to get "sober" again, at least not on the terms I had lived it for the past twenty-two years. No matter what comfort I was offered in the rooms, it was insufficient. I was no longer the man I had been, and I no longer had a solution in those chairs.

Then, I finally began to realize why I had chosen to lie and why I had avoided facing my choice to use for so long. In my mind, choosing to use was simply not OK, because on some level my identity had been based on a sober paradigm. To not be sober, was to not be me. That was flawed logic. I began to realize that for years I had subtly, but actively, judged all those around me who had used. And now I was judging myself. On some level, I felt that when I'd used, I'd betrayed who and what I was. Instead of being an ordinary human male who stumbled or fell, I was sure I must be trying to kill myself. But I wasn't really trying to kill myself. I was lost. I no longer felt I belonged in the one place I thought of as home—A.A. So in reaction, I would use, sometimes to excess, sometimes not.

Then I heard something I knew very well. Something I had heard repeated for so many years that I hardly paid attention to it anymore. It was the preamble of A.A. and it said, "The only requirement for membership was a desire to stop drinking." Like a bolt of lightning, it dawned on me that I wasn't drinking and I didn't intend to. I no longer met the primary requirement for membership. I couldn't desire to stop something I didn't desire to try. My time in A.A. was over.

After about six months of periodic slipping, I gave myself permission to explore what would happen if I simply left the rooms. I quickly learned that all I knew from A.A. came into the world with me. Over time I would see that I could choose not to use just as easily as I could choose to use (but neither choice was easy at first). In turn, experience outside the rooms allowed me to breathe deep and relax into my life.

And that's when it happened; one morning I heard myself ask the question, *"What's wrong with you?"* A smile crossed my face and the clear, clean, wonderful answer in my head, for the first time in my life, was "Nothing. Absolutely nothing."

I smiled and asked again, just to be sure. And the answer remained the same.

After that, it seemed I could finally do what A.A. had asked me to do for so long, which was to accept life on life's terms. I decided the question was the first thing that had to

202

go if I was going to succeed in doing that. I gave myself permission to experience my desires as they came. I gave myself permission to use, but rarely did. And in all this time I've had only one drink, at midnight on New Year's Eve, a glass of champagne to toast my new life. The more I allowed myself to be responsible for me, including forgiving myself for my mistakes, the less I felt I needed to use. On the random occasion when I use something other than alcohol, I usually regret the time that I have lost. I do not regret the act of using, or the experience of the escape, which I have come to understand is a fairly normal thing to want and desire. Instead I regret the loss of my faculties, the unproductive time in which I am less than my best, less sharp than the me I know. I regret the recovery period when my mind just won't work as I know it should, even if others rarely notice. The desire to not feel that dullness is enough to keep me from using with any regularity. In short, my time sober has spoiled me with clarity, and I am in no hurry to give that up. Using for all its short-term appeals is rarely worth that cost.

There are many things I learned twelve-stepping that guide me today, and those things will stay with me until I die. They are probably why I can now use with some sense of normalcy. These are things many people get from their parents or from positive socialization as young people. For me, I missed most of them until well into my twenties and some came even later. Most of these things came to me in the Program, some came from living life well, most came from my amazing family of gay men, and one absurdly special lesbian, many of whom I met in A.A.

But now that I have those things, I'm leaving the rest. For now.

After all I had been through, the scariest part was telling all the sober people who are my chosen family that I was ready to leave. But they took A.A.'s wisdom to heart and encouraged me to seek my own path. I am sure many of them expect to see me in a chair again soon. They might be right. But for now, this is what I have to do. For me and me alone.

I am, for lack of a better word, post-sober. I like this word because it evokes the power of what came before, while acknowledging that what came before is no more. For a long time, I believed I needed the program to live, or at least to survive. It was necessary daily treatment from a disease that was out to get me. As much as I once needed the program to live, the time came when I would need to live without it. In the end I would find that as much as A.A. helped me develop the skills necessary to succeed in all areas of my life, it also limited me. Over time, it had begun to re-instill the fear it had once liberated me from. Leaving A.A. was not so much a choice as a necessity, and was one of the hardest choices I have ever made.

The ultimate cure to my "spiritual malady" was found in the ability to be true to myself, regardless of the judgment of those around me. But being true to myself only works when I allow others to have the same freedom. What the program has taught me more than anything is that one of the secrets of happiness is to do my best to keep my shit out of the way of others. But in that pursuit, I no longer wish to be checked by a fellowship or a social structure. I wish to be the best, most open me possible. I wish to finally own the freedom I was promised when I entered the rooms almost a quarter century ago. As lonely as that journey may be, I finally am ready to be me, in the world, label-less.

In the end, it may be that the only thing that was ever wrong with me was the need to ask, and answer, the question. But without more than twenty years of A.A., I would have never known that.

Recovering My Sexuality
Scott Alexander Hess

The day I gave the finger to Budweiser, crack, whiskey, amyl nitrate and drug-fueled orgies, a tiny Irish man with a ravaged face and a heart the size of Alaska took my hand and quieted me as I whispered, "But what about my crazy sex life? I can't give that up."

He smiled and murmured, "You can't take a drink with a cock in your mouth."

My first thought: what if I use a straw? Luckily, I never tried that trick.

That gnome-like fellow, whom I trusted because I had no interest in fucking him and he had nothing I could steal, slowly helped me rebuild my chaotic, messy life back in the '90s. He told me to leave my sex angst on the shelf, to stay safe and sober, and that I would deal with all issues cocky when the time came.

The time came in Egypt, fifteen years later.

But first, I had to get, and stay, sober.

***

Recovery from a lifetime of abusive, booze-fueled madness has been a slow process. That first wise phrase I learned—you can't take a drink with a cock in your mouth—was soon replaced by another slogan, also suggested to me by that Irish gnome. He told me, "If you don't drink today, you are a winner!"

I thought he was nuts, but I went along with it. I had nothing to lose.

Soon I put it to the test.

To handle the rawness of living without mind-numbing booze, a lot of newly sober people distract themselves with other vices. Shopping, Häagen-Dazs, fried food. Some of my new sober friends got fat, some ran up credit cards, some smoked incessantly.

I sucked cocks. Lots of cocks.

Indeed, in my first year sober, my sexual activity ramped into overdrive. Sex momentarily quieted the anxiety that I had doused with alcohol for years. I had sex all over town with men of all shapes and sizes. One of my favorite late night pick-up haunts was a park in Brooklyn, which was near where I lived at the time. Men would linger in shadowy edges just inside the park's entrance and get each other off in the bushes. It was after one long night in the shrubs, walking home alone near dawn, that I asked myself, "How can I be stone cold sober and have sex in a public park? Am I utterly insane? A lost cause?"

I called my twelve-step sponsor, I spoke to friends, I shared vividly (perhaps too vividly!) at twelve-step meetings about these fears. Was I too fucked up to be saved?

I was told—again—"If you don't drink today, you are a winner." Half-heartedly, I believed what people told me.

Over time, I began to witness the wisdom in that phrase. I did a lot of nutty shit, but I didn't go back to using alcohol and drugs, and slowly the quality of my life greatly improved. It took time, but life got richer, fuller, and incredibly vibrant.

I began to make saner choices. I replaced my late night park prowling with the steam room sex scene at my gym (in New York, steam room sex is common). There was a numbing deadness in the steam room, a misty lack of human connection that suited me. It was similar to the dark, vacant numbness I found with alcohol-drenched oblivion.

I also began to frequent New York's West Side Club gay bathhouse. It was there, one frigid winter night in January during my fifth year of sobriety, that I made an unexpected discovery. (For bathhouse virgins, these sex clubs are sprawling, barn-like establishments with lots of small "resting cabins" for fucking. Gay men wander around in towels and get down and dirty.)

I was lounging in a public area of the bathhouse in my towel. The front desk staff played music throughout the night to keep things moving. And the song "Beautiful Freak" by the Eels came on, a moody lyrical tune. While I normally stayed sex-focused and pushed away anything close to a legitimate feeling during a romp, that song's melancholy riff caught me off guard, and I was moved by the song's brash claim that a freak can be beautiful. Momentarily, it yanked me back to boyhood, and that just pubescent boyhood yearning for love, touch, a kiss—a yearning that was so quickly destroyed by intense shame and a feeling that I was indeed a freak. It was uncanny to have such thoughts at a bathhouse, a place where sex could wipe out the world at least momentarily.

I was getting ready to call it a night and run, when a man came toward me wearing one towel around his waist and another around his head, like a turban. I recognized him as a particularly flamboyant friend I knew from a recovery meeting. He swirled straight up to me, kissed both of my cheeks, and gave me a long stare.

"What's wrong, girl?"

He said it with care, with genuine interest, and I caved in. We retreated to a corner and I blurted out a slew of pent up feelings, mostly my fear that all this anonymous sex meant I was too ruined to stay sober long-term, or become whole. I'd heard a lot of talk about the Twelve Steps, in particular step six, which supposedly helped rid you of nasty defects of character. I asked my friend flat out, "Why am I still so fucked up? Weren't these defects supposed to be lifted out of me for fuck's sake, now that I am clean?"

He adjusted his turban and smiled.

"She'll lift it when she's ready. Just don't drink girl," he said, referring to his version of God in the female form. "You are a winner."

There was that hackneyed phrase again, which in the moment, took on new meaning. It helped me take a tiny step toward self-forgiveness. I began to accept myself and simply do the best I could each day. It was all new stuff for a man who loves black and white thinking. I'm the best, I'm the worst. Go fuck yourself.

I realized that night I was flawed, I was human, and that was just fine.

***

After nine years of recovery, I fell in love with a beautiful man. Though we broke up after six years together, his cheek still rests on the edge of my heart. During that time I climbed to ecstatic highs and tumbled to neurotic lows. I learned quickly that I had a lot of trouble communicating, which ultimately led to our demise. I stayed sober, and partially sane throughout that wild emotion-charged ride, by channeling my angst into a first person diary. This was suggested to me by a therapist when I balked at the idea of anti-anxiety medication.

I did not write traditional entries. I wrote with grandiosity, in first person, always a bit dramatically, because that suited the drive of my inner voice. I suppose the episodes I began to recount, some about my infidelities during this love affair, were too painful to write "for real." I couldn't quite face what I was doing, so I wrote them as if I were creating a character. For the record, Catherine, in the Tennessee Williams' classic play *Suddenly, Last Summer* does the same thing after a lewd episode with a married man. She keeps a novelistic like diary. I imagine I subconsciously snatched the idea from her.

When the relationship ended, I went through a very bleak phase. I was fifteen-years sober, and it felt like a shot of whiskey was an inch away. My diary became a ravenous obsession. I spilled every twisted thought, obsession, fear, and perverted passion. At that time, I couldn't eat enough ice cream or fuck enough men to make an increasing anxiety go away. I realize now, this writing, these "diary" entries, were an integral part of my slow approach to clarity and healing.

There was one long winter night in particular that lead to a very unexpected catharsis.

Midnight.

I've lost track of time. There was one reject in this thus-far dreary sex binge. He was nameless, from the phone sex line, promising all sorts of muscle and hunky love. At the door to my apartment, wearing a baseball cap and leather jacket, he had the lost look of an elderly drunk who just had a stroke. His hands shook. His eyes were bleary but a pretty blue. I wanted to hug him and guide him to a hospital or rehab but I said, "Not a match," and quickly shut the door, listening to his muffled sighs and footsteps drifting slowly back down the four flights.

My three "on-the-way" tricks from Manhunt are slow, and my lids are heavy. My door buzzes. I have no idea who it is, but I buzz him up hoping for the best.

He calls himself TantricZ. He's sort of attractive with wavy red hair and a face like a worn-out Harrison Ford. He's a little chunky but well dressed.

"I only want to play with you. You don't need to touch me. Let me honor and worship your cock," he says.

I find this mildly appealing, though I realize he's not any of my three "on-the-way" Manhunt men. He may be from the phone-sex line or anywhere really. I give my address out indiscriminately. I lie back. He begins to touch me gently like a secret massage fairy that has crept out of the wall. I feel taken care of. There's a pause and I smell the stink of poppers—he's sniffing on a little bottle of amyl nitrate.

"I am your slave," he whispers.

I avoid sniffing the crap and wonder if I can get any sort of drifting contact high. I consider asking him to leave. I don't.

He's attaching something to the head of my penis. I sit up to see a tiny purple rubber circle on my cock. The rubber is attached by a thin wire to a tiny pink box. He switches it on and I am being tickled and massaged. It feels like little fingers so I lie back, but with hesitation, because this little thing is electric and he's snorting poppers again. He's mumbling something, which I begin to imagine is another language, the tantric sex slave tongue. Between the sniffing of the popper bottle up his flaring nostrils and the guttural mumbling, he is rapidly losing any scrap of appeal, piercing the tenuous fantasy bubble that keeps these slutty sessions afloat. This scent of the mundane is ruinous. I am quickly sinking to a dark place I usually only find alone in the tub. My depressive "black hole."

There is nothing worse than being in the midst of a mildly amusing sex binge and falling into my black hole.

With my eyes shut, this tingling purple thing on my penis head, and my sex slave pushing out popper scented breaths, I can more and more clearly see the edge of my black hole. I'm feeling this awful weight in my face. I suppose most people would call this being on the brink of tears, but that's not my experience. Tears are nowhere near. It's just a heaviness slowly surrounding my head. Everything in the room feels incredibly close and tight and there is this invisible suffocating scarf folding gently around my throat.

My mouth is dry, my eyes throb. The hollow of my cheeks feel full, as if I sucked in a breath underwater and took in airy water that is somehow getting thick and hard. Of course, there is no water, no scarf. It's all empty, even my cheeks and face, so I force open my eyes and confront the TantricZ man to try to get things back on a sexy track.

He's looking very closely at me. His face soft and loose, like a wave, like he's in the hole with me, as he tilts his head to one side.

"You are the saddest man I have ever seen," he says.

Then he gathers his things, gently pulls the purple contraption off of my penis, puts away his poppers, and leaves.

Things have got to get better.

2 a.m.

I'm leaning into the door, naked, stroking my penis to keep it hard with one hand and holding the peep-hole knob up with another. I cannot take another dreary man, or an old man, or a tantric slave who tells me I'm sad. If this fellow does not look promising, then I'm ditching the binge, ordering a fatty Papa John's Meat Lover's pizza and watching cartoons. I'll go to a twelve-step meeting in the morning and try to act like none of this ever happened.

211

He's from Manhunt and calls himself Jocko. Through the peep-hole he's adorable, young, masculine, and clearly a little desperate. I am studying his tiny face through the hole as he stares unwittingly ahead. I open the door. As he tentatively steps in I decide that you can determine a lot about someone through miniscule visuals.

Jocko is carrying a large duffle bag. He does not look at me, which is a relief after TantricZ. He strides in, sets down his bag, and begins to undress. We are silent. He's very orderly, folding his sweat pants, socks, and shirt on the floor by his bag. I imagine he's in his mid-twenties, and works out a lot. He is incredibly lean, with a ripple of muscle in his stomach. His hair is buzzed short.

Once undraped, he stares at me a little too long. And for a very brief second, he is a reflection of me, that dead emptiness in his eyes, that searching desperation. Luckily, he rubs his hand along his tight belly toward his crotch and I completely forget myself, which is the point. The jockstrap he wears is ratty and colored shades of gray, white, and yellow. It is loose and old and stained with what looks like years of piss, cum, and spit. His cock is bobbing inside of it quite impressively, and he's rubbing the whole package.

He nods down, and I presume he wants me to go there. So I do. It smells horrible, which disgusts and excites and challenges me. He moans ever so softly, revealing his obvious fetish for stench, so I open my mouth wide and suck on that stinky jock thing. I suck on it and make it wet, I gobble at the strap edges, I try to suck years of old gunk out of it. All the while he is moaning, and I am happy to finally find something hot and lewd. The more I suck, the more awful it tastes and smells. But the further away my black hole dissipates. I am nothing but the grossness of this jock and his lean young hands on my head pushing me back and forth. I love the vileness of this *thing in my mouth. It's absolutely liberating. I want this to go on and on, and it does for quite a while.*

Then he abruptly pushes me away and motions to the sofa. I lie down on it. He's fishing inside his duffle, and I have my usual "could there be a chainsaw in there like in American Psycho *moment. But I become intrigued as he pulls out six different jock straps and three sport cups.*

I am not athletic in the team joining sense, and have never even seen a cup. In fantasy, I have imagined hockey players or football studs shoving cups over their huge cock baskets. He comes at me quickly now, all hesitation and gentleness gone, as he puts a white hard athletic cup over my face. I think of that oxygen mask that drops from the hatch above you on a crashing airplane and also of a Ken doll's curved smooth plastic genitals. The cup fits nicely over my nose and mouth and smells funky, but nothing like his putrid jock. He begins to play with my cock, as he holds the cup on my mouth. He is grunting and I imagine he's happy. I'm enjoying the multiple sensations, the musky smell of the cup, his hands on me.

I would like to kiss him, but he seems very much in control now, so I dare not be too bold. He removes the cup and replaces it with another, this one sheathed inside an "armor gear" jock strap, which seems larger than the usual type; maybe for super well-endowed rugby players. He's pushing it roughly onto my face and it's pressing uncomfortably into my cheek, but I don't want to complain because I never want him to leave. I shut my eyes and let him push the cup harder and harder into my face and I try to suck deeper because I think he would like this. I inhale steadily and think of the novel I snuck into my parent's barn and read, The Story of O*. I also think of the S/M film,* 9½ Weeks *starring Kim Bassinger and a pre-face-lifted Mickey Rourke. Sucking on the cup, I decide that all of these characters shared a deep love.*

I hope Jocko stays for a full day or two and overwhelms my life. The cup has cut into my cheek, and tiny drops of blood creep up out of my skin. Blood trickles onto the cup's white plastic. It is obviously a wildly erotic trigger for Jocko because he immediately climaxes, shooting his cum on my belly without uttering a sound. He pulls the cup away, examining it like a precious jewel, wiping away all traces of blood with another jock strap. Then he dresses, packs his duffle, and never looking at me, quickly exits.

I lie there, sad yet content, realizing that nobody ever really says good-bye properly.

Dawn

A final desperate search on Manhunt has landed a real life Thor at my door. He stumbles in and quickly strips. He is clearly fucked up, but I justify that getting this over with will allow me to sleep, clear my head, get to a twelve-step meeting, get on with my life.

Standing nude before me, Thor is big and brawny-muscled, chiseled cheek-bones, collagen lips, a perfect moon ass, and a really huge cock. I'm not used to Latino porn star-style hook ups, so I figure I've hit papi pay dirt. Somehow this will get me back on track. This will resolve my despair.

Wrong.

Thor drops down, lying like a perfect sculpture on the floor of my kitchenette. He begins to moan and thrash about, looking up at me. His moans swiftly shift from "oh yeah man" to "fuck me, fuck me, with your foot, fuck me with anything, fuck me with a butter knife. Now!"

I swear his eyes are rolling back in his head as I think to hide my new Macy's cutlery. The moment freezes as I tower over him, briefly stunned.

214

The sun has without invitation begun to slip through the small window in my kitchenette. It's morning. Thor acrobatically yanks his legs over his head and begins to aggressively spread his perfect ass cheeks and mutter, "Get something, hurry, a dildo, a knife. Hurry, come on, man, do it, please. I gotta feel it up there!"

I stand still. I can't move. I know that desperate need, and I feel the hated dawn licking at me through the kitchenette window, both now and years ago, when I just couldn't stay drunk or high long enough or escape far enough, and I see in this mad dog, drugged up man's face, the soulless longing we share and how he wants to obliterate the world, and I suddenly, in a bizarre flash, remember a trip I took to Egypt.

I was standing on the deck of a riverboat slugging down the Nile, staring at a group of boys washing their clothes on the shore. It was 110 degrees as the sun set, and I was aware of an emerging, deeply hidden fear. That fear had just been brought to the surface by an Egyptian bellhop who had suggested a three-way with me and my then-lover.

Thor is weeping now, and a door that had opened and been abruptly shut in Egypt is drifting open again. I remember looking at my then-lover and a fawn-like bellhop in the state room, thinking, They want to have a three way. *At the time I thought,* I can't do that with a man I love, with a man who knows me. I can do it with strangers, I can become someone else, I can keep it hidden but I can't do it with a man I love.

I fled the room on that Nile riverboat, and ran to the boat's roof, spinning with some vague realization— I had a new opportunity to begin to talk honestly with my lover for the first time in our relationship. But as quickly as that all opened up, I shut it down.

My lover and I broke up soon after the trip.

Thor is sitting up and I've gotten him a glass of

*water. He tells me, wild eyed and strangely giddy, about
the men he's had sex with tonight, and the meth he had
shot into his cock. He seems to be experiencing a moment
of clarity, and I tell him about my years off of drugs and
how my life has changed, and I give him my number and
he leaves.*

*I wonder if my recovery sponsor would consider this
twelve-step work. My apartment is lit with daylight as I try
to fall asleep, and cannot.*

***

It would be nice to say that my wild sex binge with
Thor was the end, and I began to change. But mine is not a
nice story. It is a flawed, awkward, messy, and an often
brutal journey toward my unique brand of personal
sobriety. I recently celebrated eighteen-years clean and
sober, and I'm grateful for every blistering second of my
journey.

The joy is that with enough time and clarity from
years of sober living, I am slowly able to open myself to
the type of awakening that was offered to me with a
mildly nutty meth head. Seeing my own pain in Thor's
face helped me begin to find clarity.

After that weekend, I did a few precise things. I wrote
those very detailed journal entries, and I shared them with
a sober man I trusted. I also began to write more and more
specifically about my sexual experiences, particularly the
most lascivious and shameful ones. This inner venting and
constant writing led me back toward a love of prose which
I had thought was long dead. I decided to attend graduate
school in New York (The New School) and pursue an
MFA in fiction writing. Slowly, in graduate school, I
began to evolve my sexual escapades, both real and
imagined, into prose. My journal entries were the initial

spark that led to my writing my first novel, *Diary of a Sex Addict*.

After writing for a while, I was able to speak to my ex-lover and make amends about things I did when we were together, things I had long hidden and been afraid to face. I did not stop having crazy sex hook ups, but I began to see my choices in every tryst. What was most wondrous for me was that I began to reveal myself to other men. No matter what the situation—butt naked with a stranger in my apartment or at a movie theater on a date— I began to show my fuller self. I stopped hiding. And that has made a world of difference.

***

Water has always been pivotal in my journey. Bubble baths to stop myself from slipping into my black hole, moments of clarity on the Nile, and more recently meditative trips to the shore.

Last summer, standing naked at the lip of a silvery dawn ocean on a deserted Fire Island beach, I felt a part of myself momentarily drift away. I was staying for a week in a rented studio, a vacation I'd initially dreamt would be for my lover and myself. The trip was a melancholy one.

Standing nude at the water's edge, I was acutely aware of my body. From a distance, a man ambled toward me walking his dog. Nudity had always been a first step toward sex. Even alone, late at night, undressing, the mere act of being nude triggered a need in me to be touched, to relieve some ancient nagging that could start me hunting for cock. At that moment, at the water, I felt a strange sense of calm, and a freedom in being naked, facing an immense foamy swell, not needing anything from myself or anyone else. There was nothing to run from. I wasn't turned on and I wasn't ashamed.

I felt sensual, as the water rushed up my legs and tickled my thighs. I felt fully in my body. The man passed slowly with his dog, and I smiled—an honest smile.

Then I walked steadily into the waves and dove in.

Appendix A:
Additional Resources for Living Sober

At NYU's Center for Health, Identity, Behavior and Prevention Studies, under the leadership of Associate Dean Dr. Perry Halkitis, CDC and NIH funded studies have produced literally hundreds of articles on the topic of addiction and the complex nature by which it is intertwined with sexual and cultural identities. Other academic centers like this one around the world continue to research and publish findings that suggest addiction and alcoholism are complex life-long and life-threatening issues, and that A.A. and "The Twelve Steps" are not the right solution for everyone. But these academic findings rarely transfer into practical treatment applications. Despite a great amount of theoretical writing and research, only a few alternatives to A.A. and the Twelve Steps exist.

There are currently only a few formally structured alternative treatments for the very wealthy, such as the California-based Passages treatment center. Amazon.com even offers a "Top Ten Best Alternatives to A.A. List," which offers bestselling self help-literature. Other groups like Secular Organizations for Sobriety, Moderation Management, LifeRing Secular Recovery, Rational Recovery, and SMART Recovery (Self-Management and Recovery Training) call themselves self-empowerment programs. They focus on helping an individual feel powerful instead of requiring that they admit powerlessness.

With the overarching self-empowering perspective, each of these programs has their own version of A.A.'s "principles," like those found in SMART Recovery, which says that it:

- Teaches tools for recovery based on evidence-based addiction treatment
- Does not use the labels "addict" or "alcoholic"
- Encourages participation only for as long as it is perceived to be useful
- Allows for truly anonymous participation via a screen name on the website
- Allows participants their own perspective on whether addiction is a disease
- Teaches tools for recovery that are useful regardless of what the participant believes (or not) about God
- Accepts the validity of appropriately prescribed addiction and psychiatric medication.

These self-empowerment programs all claim to be gay-friendly and are gaining in popularity in the world but remain slow starts within the gay community. At first glance this might appear that it is because the twelve-step model is so widely accepted in our gay culture. It may also be because more extreme using requires a more extreme response.

The movement that has the most traction in the gay community is the Harm Reduction Coalition, which focuses less on abstinence and more on using practical methods to reduce the harm of using. Harm Reduction groups and therapists practicing this method exist in most major cities. But Harm Reduction is not a formal treatment program; rather it's a philosophy, usually applied in cognitive-based therapy, when such resources are available. Harm Reduction may prove to be a viable alternative to complete abstinence, but its theories and practices are not widely accepted. The Harm Reduction Coalition website outlines its "principles" as follows:

Harm reduction is a set of practical strategies and ideas aimed at reducing negative consequences associated with drug use. Harm Reduction is also a movement for social justice built on a belief in, and respect for, the rights of people who use drugs.

Harm reduction incorporates a spectrum of strategies from safer use, to managed use to abstinence to meet drug users "where they're at," addressing conditions of use along with the use itself. Because harm reduction demands that interventions and policies designed to serve drug users reflect specific individual and community needs, there is no universal definition of or formula for implementing harm reduction.

However, HRC considers the following principles central to harm reduction practice:

- *Accepts, for better and or worse, that licit and illicit drug use is part of our world and chooses to work to minimize its harmful effects rather than simply ignore or condemn them*
- *Understands drug use as a complex, multi-faceted phenomenon that encompasses a continuum of behaviors from severe abuse to total abstinence, and acknowledges that some ways of using drugs are clearly safer than others*
- *Establishes quality of individual and community life and well-being–not necessarily cessation of all drug*

221

use–as the criteria for successful interventions and policies

- *Calls for the non-judgmental, non-coercive provision of services and resources to people who use drugs and the communities in which they live in order to assist them in reducing attendant harm*
- *Ensures that drug users and those with a history of drug use routinely ha.ve a real voice in the creation of programs and policies designed to serve them*
- *Affirms drugs users themselves as the primary agents of reducing the harms of their drug use, and seeks to empower users to share information and support each other in strategies which meet their actual conditions of use*
- *Recognizes that the realities of poverty, class, racism, social isolation, past trauma, sex-based discrimination and other social inequalities affect both people's vulnerability to and capacity for effectively dealing with drug-related harm*
- *Does not attempt to minimize or ignore the real and tragic harm and danger associated with licit and illicit drug use*

Harm Reduction philosophies are growing in popularity, but face abstinence-based controversy akin to passing out condoms in public schools. Harm Recduction literature, which frequently outlines topics like "How to avoid an opioid overdose," is often aimed at saving the life of the hardcore drug user, and as a result its methods are often accused of promoting drug use rather than preventing it.

As a result, the Twelve Steps created in A.A. remain the go-to resource for treatment and recovery for anyone experiencing a problem with addictive behaviors.

Other Gay Friendly 12-Step Resources

12StepRadio.com. An online radio station that features sober music and talk radio. http://12stepradio.com

Al-Anon Family Groups. The parent group of Ala-non and Ala-teen. Provides resources for families living with an alcoholic or addict.
http://www.al-anon.alateen.org

Alcoholics...Anonymous...Intergroup. Provides compre-hensive lists and time of active meetings. Lists international resources as well. Check your local listings for a phone number, or try http://www.A.A..org

Alcoholics Anonymous (2001). Alcoholics Anonymous, 4th Edition. New York: A.A. World Services. The Big Book. Available via most booksellers or download it for free at http://www.A.A..org/bigbookonline

"A.A Fact File." An A.A. published pamphlet that provides on overview of the group, its membership and its structure. Downloadable via
www.A.A..org/pdf/products/m-24_A.A.factfile.pdf

Crystal Meth Anonymous Intergroup. Provides connec-tions with local resources. Hotline: 855-638-4383. http://www.crystalmeth.org

Gal-A.A. (Gays and Lesbians in Alcoholics Anonymous). Established to serve and have the involvement of the lesbians, gay men, and gay people in Alcoholics Anonymous, regardless of how they chose to identify themselves. Website lists upcoming round-up events. http://gal-A.A..org

Gay and Lesbian Community Center. Find yours local center via www.Centerlink.org or by emailing: CenterLink@lgbtcenters.org

Sober Round-ups. These locally hosted "gay sober conventions" feature workshops, speakers and literature on the topic of being sober and gay. Dates, times and durations vary from city to city, but all are welcome. Many sober gays vacation to these weekends. See Gal-A.A.

"Information on Alcoholics Anonymous." Pamphlet. Download for free at http://www.A.A..org/pdf/products/f-2_InfoonA.A..pdf

Intervention America, National Resource of America. Provides comprehensive listings of Drug Rehabs in the US. 888-629-3330. http://interventionamerica.org

Lambda. This is a common name for locally funded and managed sober twelve-step meetings and/or meeting centers for gay and lesbian twelve-step groups. Centers exist in Dallas, Houston, Ft. Lauderdale. Miami/Dade. New Orleans. Palm Beach. Phoenix. Sacramento, and many others. Check your local twelve-step Intergroup meeting listings.

Pride Institute. For over twenty-five years this center has provided GLBT focused addition recovery. Located in Minneapolis and Ft. Lauderdale. http://www.pride-institute.com

Other Gay-Friendly Resources on Addiction and Recovery

2-1-1. Dial 2-1-1 on almost any phone in the US for a local comprehensive health and human services referrals. Check the 2-1-1 website for service areas and local information. www.211.org

Addictionsandrecovery.org. A website that looks at various forms of addiction and recovery. http://www.addictionsandrecovery.org

Allaboutaddiction.com. A website and blog dedicated to issues about addiction. Includes a rehab-finder. http://www.allaboutaddiction.com/

Center for Addiction Management. Dr. John Fitzgerald's blog and website for addiction management. http://addictionmanagement.org/

Facebook. Many city-based and regional sober groups exist. Search for "Sober" followed the name of your city. Try the same for Harm Reduction and SMART Recovery. http://facebook.com

"The Fix, Addition and Recovery, Straight Up." Provides articles and blogger who report on the trials of sober living. Also connects people with rehab and sober living facilities. Hotline: 888-GET-FIXED. http://www.thefix.com

Harm Reduction Coalition Website. The online presence of the largest organization of Harm Reduction Academics and Professionals. http://harmreduction.org

Huffington Post Addiction and Recovery. This popular political blog also contains a section on Addition and recovery. http://huffingtonpost.com

Kink Aware Professionals Directory. Hosted by the National Coalition for Sexual Freedom. Referrals to psychotherapeutic, medical, legal and other professionals who are knowledgeable about and sensitive to diverse expressions of sexuality. (410) 539-4824 Kap@ncsfreedom.org. https://ncsfreedom.org/home-mainmenu-1.html

LifeRing Secular Recovery. LifeRing is a network of support groups for people who have learned through experience that the only solution that works is to abstain completely. Through the positive reinforcement of the group process, that power to be sober becomes dominant in each person and enables them to lead clean and sober lives. The website provides information about the group, including frequently asked questions, publications, an online forum area for support, and links to local meetings. http://www.unhooked.com/index.htm

Moderation Management. A "mutual-help organization" which promotes self-management, balance, moderation and responsibility. Utilizes an email listserv. http://www.moderation.org

The Pennsylvania Model. Pennsylvania Model is the use of medication, such as Naltrexone, in addition to Cognitive Behavioral Therapy, Motivational Enhancement Therapy and/or Rational Emotive Behavior Therapy. Alcohol abuse is treated as a bio-psycho-social condition, rather than a "spiritual disease". Assisted Recovery Centers of America (ARCA) was the first in the nation to offer a non 12-step program of recovery using this model. http://www.assistedrecovery.com/beta/pen.htm

Rational Recovery. A worldwide source of counseling, guidance, and direct instruction on self-recovery from addiction to alcohol and other drugs through planned, permanent abstinence. The group believes that individuals are on their own in staying sober, so there are no meetings or treatment centers as part of the approach, nor is there any counseling, therapy, psychology or spirituality. The website provides information about the method (Addictive Voice Recognition Technique® (AVRT®)), frequently asked questions, free information for those trying to stay sober, as well as their families, and information about subscription based services. http://www.rational.org

Recovery is Everywhere. A website dedicated to reducing the stigma of addiction.
http://recoveryiseverywhere.com

Secular Organizations for Recovery. SOS Recovery. A west coast based secular and scientific alternative to A.A. email: sos@cfiwest.org.
http://www.cfiwest.org/sos/index.htm

SMART Recovery (Self-Management and Recovery Training). A group cognitive/behavioral based 12-step alternative. http://www.smartrecovery.org

Stop, Drop, Recover. A daily blog of inspirational quotes and resources for sober people.
http://stopdroprecover.blogspot.com

"So You'd Like to Know the Top Ten Alternatives to A.A." Amazon.com. This list updates alternative sobriety

books based Amazon sales.
http://www.amazon.com/gp/richpub/syltguides/fullview/R
HK90RB6134X6

Sober Bloggers Directory. An online directory of sober bloggers. www.soberblogs.gotop100.com/

Treatment4addiction.com Online Recovery Resources Directory. A blog reportedly written by addiction recovery professionals. Hotline 888-781-7840.
http://www.treatment4addiction.com/blog

Queer+Sober. This NYC based event promoter aims its circuit-like parties at the clean and sober crowd.
http://nycqueerandsober.org

Year of Sober Living. A blog that examines the first year of sobriety. www.yearofsoberliving.com

Appendix B:
The Twelve Steps of Alcoholics Anonymous

1. We admitted we were powerless over alcohol—that our lives had become unmanageable.
2. Came to believe that a Power greater than ourselves could restore us to sanity.
3. Made a decision to turn our will and our lives over to the care of God *as we understood Him.*
4. Made a searching and fearless moral inventory of ourselves.
5. Admitted to God, to ourselves, and to another human being the exact nature of our wrongs.
6. Were entirely ready to have God remove all these defects of character.
7. Humbly asked Him to remove our shortcomings.
8. Made a list of all persons we had harmed, and became willing to make amends to them all.
9. Made direct amends to such people wherever possible, except when to do so would injure them or others.
10. Continued to take personal inventory and when we were wrong promptly admitted it.
11. Sought through prayer and meditation to improve our conscious contact with God, *as we understood Him*, praying only for knowledge of His will for us and the power to carry that out.
12. Having had a spiritual awakening as the result of these

Steps, we tried to carry this message to alcoholics, and to practice these principles in all our affairs.

Appendix C:
The Twelve Traditions of Alcoholics Anonymous

1. Our common welfare should come first; personal recovery depends upon A.A. unity.
2. For our group purpose there is but one ultimate authority — a loving God as He may express Himself in our group conscience. Our leaders are but trusted servants; they do not govern.
3. The only requirement for A.A. membership is a desire to stop drinking.
4. Each group should be autonomous except in matters affecting other groups or A.A. as a whole.
5. Each group has but one primary purpose—to carry its message to the alcoholic who still suffers.
6. An A.A. group ought never endorse, finance or lend the A.A. name to any related facility or outside enterprise, lest problems of money, property and prestige divert us from our primary purpose.
7. Every A.A. group ought to be fully self-supporting, declining outside contributions.
8. Alcoholics Anonymous should remain forever nonprofessional, but our service centers may employ special workers.
9. A.A., as such, ought never be organized; but we may create service boards or committees directly responsible to those they serve.

10. Alcoholics Anonymous has no opinion on outside issues; hence the A.A. name ought never be drawn into public controversy.
11. Our public relations policy is based on attraction rather than promotion; we need always maintain personal anonymity at the level of press, radio and films.
12. Anonymity is the spiritual foundation of all our traditions, ever reminding us to place principles before personalities.

Acknowledgements

As anonymity is a definitive and very personal part of twelve-step structure, it becomes a complex thing to create acknowledgements for this book. Clearly I owe a debt to the contributors. Their stories, stumbles, and triumphs are the heart of this book. I thank them all for endless patience through what seemed to be an almost never-ending process. And I owe a debt to Don Weise at Magnus Books, who stood by this idea, and never failed to believe in my ability to execute it, through a great many ups and downs. He was always determined to see this book through to publication.

I can clearly state that my time at NYU's Stienhardt, and my personal relationship with Dr. Perry Halkitis, have influenced this book and its content beyond measure. His work, and the work of his students at the Center for Health, Identity, Behavior and Prevention Studies, greatly altered my ideas about addiction and are laying the groundwork for the way the world will see these issues in the future. Further, my professors and fellow students at NYU/Steinhardt, especially Niobe Way, Nan Smithner, Joe Salvatore, and Teresa Fisher, who each in their own way helped open my mind to all that it was capable of understanding, as well as the capacity I had for feeling compassion for others. In turn, I was able to apply that capacity toward my own self-improvement.

I also owe a debt to Elizabeth Williams, Peggy Rajski, Donna Galeno, and Rosemary Calderalo. These women each saw more in me than I ever saw in myself, and taught me what I was capable of. Elizabeth and Rosemary's faith and encouragement have especially seen me through challenging periods that made me I think I had nothing left. These two women taught me that is almost never the case. Each member of this foursome afforded me opportunities to try, and do, in ways for which I will be forever grateful.

Beyond that, this is an exercise in respecting the anonymity of others. There are five sober gay people that I think of as my family. I could have never made it through the last twenty-plus years without their advice and counsel. As the Twelve Steps taught me to do, I will tell them each, one-by-one, how they are responsible for this book and its development. Many other great ideas and thoughts in this book have been picked up "in the rooms" and are, by tradition, attributed to no one. And that's OK too.

About the Editor

Leslie L. Smith has produced, written and directed independent film and off-Broadway. His feature film, *David Searching* was accepted to the Outfest Legacy Project/UCLA Film Archive. His first novel *Sally Field Can Play the Transexual* is forthcoming. His work in social services includes strategic planning for 9/11 Recovery and the Trevor Project. Visit him online at http://www.leslielsmith.com.

About the Contributors

Jim B. was born, raised, and educated amidst the cornfields of Illinois. A lover of language and languages, men, Dolly, books, and food, reading, writing, walking, and learning, he writes, loves, and lives in Paris.

Jay C. has been sober since August 8, 1987. He is a documentary filmmaker and multimedia producer. He lives in New York City with his husband.

Mike C. chooses to remain anonymous.

Edge is an author and teacher from Florida with twenty-five years of experience in the leather scene. He's equally passionate about his recovery, which he continues to pursue as he enters his eighth year of sobriety.

Wayne H. is forty-six, living in an overpriced but rent-stabilized apartment in Manhattan for the last seventeen years, petless and plantless. He is thrilled to be published for the first time,and happy to report being in his first successful, adult, sober, and monogamous relationship. He is still a meeting-maker.

Scott Alexander Hess's debut novel *Diary of a Sex Addict* is "relentlessly erotic and divinely written" (Richard Labonte, *Bookmarks*). His other work: the novels *Bergdorf*

Boys, *The Jockey*, and *Three Brothers*. He co-wrote the film *Tom in America* starring Sally Kirkland and Burt Young. He blogs for the Huffington Post. Visit him online at http://www.scottalexanderhess.com.

R.J. Hughes was a longtime reporter for the *Wall StreetJournal*. He is the author of several novels, including the acclaimed *LateandSoon*, and a forthcoming play. He lives in New York and Paris.

Peter Joshua is an award-winning American writer, editor and executive at a media company. He lives in rural Connecticut and New York. He is a passionate if untalented fly fisherman, gardener, and an excellent cook. He is a loving father and uncle, and keeps meaning to get back to the gym.

Frank Turrentine is a fifty-year-old part-time farmer engaging in permaculture experiments on the banks of the Brazos River in north central Texas. He currently spends his time planting trees and playing with his dog and intermittently reading good books when the weather forces him indoors.

Chris Steele is from Dallas, Texas. He has been a member of A.A. since November of 1988. His career choices proved to be controversial both in and out of A.A. He has worked as a gay bartender, a gay bar manager, a gay porn star, and finally a gay porn producer.

N.H.W. has lived in New York City for twelve years. Currently, he is an active member of several twelve-step fellowships, where he holds service positions and sponsors men in recovery. He works in financial services and is pursuing a MBA. He is engaged, has two dogs and does remix/production work for leisure.

Made in the USA
Lexington, KY
08 November 2016